COMING OF AGE
WITH THE JESUITS

COMING OF AGE
WITH THE JESUITS

Mark J. Curran

Order this book online at www.trafford.com
or email orders@trafford.com

Most Trafford titles are also available at major online book retailers.

Cover, "Rockhurst Magazine," Fall, 2001.
Image Courtesy of Rockhurst University, Office of Public Relations and Marketing

Printed in the United States of America.

ISBN: 978-1-4669-2234-1 (sc)
ISBN: 978-1-4669-2235-8 (e)

Library of Congress Control Number: 2012906069

Trafford rev. 04/19/2012

 www.trafford.com

North America & international
toll-free: 1 888 232 4444 (USA & Canada)
phone: 250 383 6864 ♦ fax: 812 355 4082

For classmates and friends from Rockhurst College and Saint Louis University and the faculty, both Jesuit and lay. Please accept my thanks and deepest appreciation.

Contents

List of Illustrations

Cover of the book. Cover, "Rockhurst Magazine," Fall, 2001.
Image Courtesy of Rockhurst University, Office of Public Relations and Marketing

Back cover of the book. Mark, Classical Guitar, St. Bartholomew's Catholic Church, Bayfield, Colorado

PREFACE

Like "The Farm," the story of growing up on a small Kansas wheat farm in the 1940s and 1950s, an account dedicated to my parents and family and to a lesser extent to childhood school friends from those days, this book too is about memories. In a sense it is a continuation of "The Farm." Although autobiographical in nature, it is much more. The book is a recollection of seven years spent in Jesuit schools of higher learning. It is meant to not only relive those days, but tell what Jesuit education was like during the early and mid-1960s. The story is not unusual, yet perhaps not typical since I was a product of public schools in Kansas and not the Jesuit prep school or big city Catholic high school of so many of my Rockhurst friends.

The story will be told chronologically but the memory is in charge. The narration is based on a list of persons, places and events written down years after the fact and then recounted in the various sections of the book. I apologize now for the lack of more precise details but it has been a long time. The book is once again a change of pace from academic writing. Since I'm not gifted in the art of fiction, these short "chronicles" are a compilation of what happened and what I thought about it.

In addition to the two phases of Jesuit education, the first at then Rockhurst College in Kansas City, Missouri, and the latter at Saint Louis University in St. Louis, Missouri, sandwiched between is the telling of my first encounter with Latin America leading to a future career of language and culture teaching at Arizona State University. My first foreign experience took place the summer between junior and senior years at Rockhurst and was spent studying at the National University of Mexico in Mexico City followed by travels in Mexico and Guatemala.

The book is illustrated with personal photos, but I am in debt to images scanned from "Rockhurst Magazine" and "The Saint Louis University Calendar, 2012," and images used with permission from the Office of Archives, Saint Louis University. Credits will be given accordingly.

Finally, the book is certainly not an academic or historic treatise on the Jesuits or their philosophy of education, the "Ratio Studiorum," but rather a personal account of a young man's formative years with them. Thus it comes in the wrappings of the memories of a nineteen-year-old with feelings of nervousness in the beginning, a bit of fright at the Jesuit discipline and ways, and a whole lot of immaturity. Was this typical? Perhaps yes. A title could have just as easily been "Growing Up with the Jesuits." There was some maturation that took place in those seven years, but it was just the beginning. All was not assistance at mass, toil, study and cramming for exams, not by a long shot. I hope the reader can share the memories.

PART I.
UNDERGRADUATE DAYS
AT A JESUIT SCHOOL

Cover of "Rockhurst Magazine, Fall, 2001"
Image Courtesy of Rockhurst University, Office of Public Relations and Marketing

A. THE FIRST YEAR

1. The Beginnings

After graduation from public high school in Abilene, Kansas, in 1959, it was expected that I would go on to college, following in the footsteps of my two older brothers and sister. As I said in "The Farm," an earlier book about growing up on a small family wheat farm near Abilene, Kansas, and school days in the 1940s and 1950s, our family is of Irish extraction and always lived the Catholic religion that goes with it. When time for college came, Catholic schools were the priority. Oldest brother Jim attended a Jesuit institution, Creighton University in Omaha, Nebraska, for two years on the G.I. Bill after serving in the Army Air Corps in WW II. Sister Jo Anne after trying her luck at Kansas State University and the sorority system transferred to Mary Mount College in Salina, Kansas, a school administrated by the St. Joseph nuns, and graduated two years later. My brother Tom garnered a Naval ROTC scholarship at a Jesuit school, Marquette University in Milwaukee, and would go on to graduate in four years and serve on active duty in the navy as an officer, serving on a "Tin Can," the destroyer Charles Brown, affectionately known as the "Charlie Brown." I believe it was my mother, a brave schoolmarm in the one room rural schools of Colorado and Kansas in the 1920s and 1930s, an educator herself, who had great admiration for the Jesuits and their schools; Dad never said much about it at all. My only exposure to the Jesuits prior to college was the annual parish church mission during lent in Abilene in the 1950s when they invited a Jesuit probably from nearby St. Mary's Seminary for the fire and brimstone services during Holy Week.

So I borrowed my brother Jim's 1959 Mercedes Diesel Sedan and drove to Omaha during senior year in high school to take the entrance exam for Creighton. I flat out flunked it; I surmise, because the science and math were nothing but a mystery to me. I knew what the results would be when I walked out of the exam room.

The next step turned out to be an application to a smaller Jesuit school, Rockhurst College in Kansas City, Missouri. They accepted my excellent high school grades and perhaps SAT scores and admitted me for the fall of 1959. Why Rockhurst? The son of one of Mom's church lady friends, Bill Hough, attended Rockhurst years earlier and graduated there before entering the priesthood. I think it was that recommendation that influenced Mom's choice. A state university like Kansas State or Kansas University or Washburn University in Topeka were discussed, options most of my high school friends were to take, but I readily accepted the Rockhurst decision, but probably for all the wrong reasons.

Mark J. Curran

In high school in Abilene the biggest treat for local small town country kids was a trip to Kansas City, Missouri. My brother Jim took me there in 1955 when I saw my first major league baseball game. The view of that splendid green field and huge stadium at 22nd Street and Brooklyn awed me, and the Kansas City Athletics, a pretty lousy team at the time, was not the point: it was the opposition. At various times I would see one of Ted Williams' last games (he went four for four, a homer, a double and two singles) and Mickey Mantle, my greatest hero (he slugged at least one home run that time). So Kansas City brought this possibility. On another trip to the city with guys from the high school class of 59, we stayed at a small hotel downtown, drank some beer and went to a real burlesque show on 12th street, probably in one of the last burlesque theaters in the U.S.A. Then we went to a ball game.

And Kansas City had the Plaza, the beautiful shopping area south of downtown; coincidentally Rockhurst was not far off, at 55th and Troost, the Plaza on 48th if I recall.

So trusting Mom's view that the Jesuits were fine educators, and I was ignorant of their origin and history at that time, and that Rockhurst had a good reputation, and liking the idea of Kansas City, I went ahead and planned for that option. An aside from later days: I do not know why, but Notre Dame with all its fame and reputation, was never discussed by me or by my parents. It was just not in the mix. Being a bit wiser today, I rather doubt I would have passed their entrance exam either, but my grades and academic record might have swayed that decision. I am sure we would not have had the resources for Notre Dame. To me at the time it was just this big Catholic school with a famous football team.

So with Mom and Dad initially paying most of my expenses, this after working for Dad on the farm for many summers for future college expenses, including the summer following graduation from Abilene High School in May, 1959, in September they delivered me to the dorm at Rockhurst. It was exciting, and I was anxious to start this new phase in life. The goodbye was sad, but it was agreed I would come home at Thanksgiving, just a few months away.

2.   Arrival at Rockhurst

Mark, Keah, Conway Hall, Rockhurst University, 2000

Goodbyes were said to my parents and I was shown to my room in the dormitory, Xavier-Loyola Hall, a room to be shared with one other person. The first roommate was Phil Kezele from Gallup, New Mexico, who in fact took the train to school, Gallup still being a major rail stop way out west. We were to become friends if not great friends later. All I recall is that before going to bed we both talked about how we liked music, so the damned music he played on the radio kept me up all night. The next day, by mutual consent I think, I switched to the roommate who would be with me for the next two years, Irish-Catholic Jim Fitzgerald from the small Kansas town of Concordia, not far from Abilene, whose teams we played in athletics.

The dormitory was rather new with three or four floors of rooms. In the center was the lobby, some easy chairs and divans, a place for anyone to wait for their son, etc. And the pay telephones! There were no telephones in the rooms and obviously none of the electronics of fifty years later. Rockhurst was not co-educational, so the dorms were for men only. On either side of the lobby there were two wings with the dorm rooms, and in the basement there was a TV room, cigarette machine, pool tables and a lounge area to read magazines or just shoot the bull. The cigarette machine comes in to play: I recall very clearly walking up to it, depositing 30 cents and buying a pack of Viceroys, thinking I'm on my own and this is what I want to do. It would be the beginning of 12-15 years of steady cigarette smoking.

The dorm room was neatly divided in half, the same accoutrements for each of two boys. There was a single bed with sheets, pillow and blankets, the sheets you turned in each Saturday a.m. for fresh new ones. There was a small closet for hanging clothes and a bureau with several drawers to the side. Above the bureau were a mirror and an electric plug in. At the other end of the bed was the study desk with book shelves above. It was all quite adequate and I certainly never required more than that. A fair amount of the desk top was taken by my new Smith-Corona Electric Typewriter, a graduation gift and the tool I used most in college. My Sears-Roebuck classic guitar, bought through the Sears catalogue for $50 earned from work at the Abilene Ice Plant, was stowed beneath the single bed, but would be hauled out regularly later on.

In the center of the room between the two desks was a fairly large window looking out to the street. I would live in such a room for the four years at Rockhurst and beyond that for three and one-half years at Saint Louis University. I never ever thought of getting an apartment or renting a room in a house off campus. My job was to study and with few complications as possible. Cafeteria food would be adequate if not particularly tasty; it was a close walk to classes, sports games, etc. Life was simple and good.

On each floor of the dorm there was a student resident, probably a junior or senior, and a priest in residence at the end of the hall. They checked into any shenanigans. I never had a problem with them at all, but you knew they were there.

And of course all meals were served in the student cafeteria up the hill. You got in line, grabbed a tray and silverware, filled the tray, and sat down at a table with friends. This went on three times a day for four years. Memories are hazy; the food was adequate if not especially tasty. I never complained much; it was the way it was done. Eat and get back to the room to study or whatever. The food staff did institute a "steak night" during junior or senior year; that was a pleasure. I recall the meals, lots of cigarettes and coffee afterwards, and one particularly fateful evening. News came of the Cuban Missile Crisis, all of us on pins and needles; we were sure we either would be destroyed by nuclear bombs, or at the least drafted into the military for the coming war with the Soviet Union.

Back to my roommate Jim Fitzgerald. We really got along well, and I don't ever remember getting into a fight or argument with him; credit perhaps goes to him as much as to me. We were indeed different. Jim was tall, maybe 6 ft. 3, not heavy or fat, but totally un-athletic. He dressed extremely well for a college student — expensive dress slacks, dress shirts, sweaters, and many sport coats and suits and ties. On weekends he might spend a Saturday at the Plaza buying ever more clothes. He was just an average student, but I think garnered his B's and Cs. His family was fairly well off, his father with a big hardware store in Concordia. Jim, as I said, was un-athletic but was the student manager for the basketball team at Concordia high school and a good sports fan. We attended many of the college basketball games, Rockhurst being a strong NAIA school. Aside from all the time in the room and the cafeteria and a few classes in common, one other activity we did share was the Friday night beer blasts soon to take place on the Kansas side. Jim had an uncle in K.C. and it was a weekly occurrence for Jim to join him for dinner at a high end restaurant. He never ever "lorded" his apparent money over me, not once. Jim was great fun at the tavern and would tell Irish jokes and sing old Irish favorites. The one I recall most was "Who Put the Overalls in Mrs. Murphy's Chowder," a song I would learn 40 years later for playing in a bar-restaurant in Durango, Colorado.

A minor point of the dorm living was laundry, thus my small anecdote. Dear ole' Mom had sent me off to Rockhurst with a small "suitcase" of plastic I think. It was the same laundry box that my oldest brother Jim had used at Creighton University after World War II, ostensibly to send laundry home. Did Jim actually ship this box from Omaha, Nebraska, to Abilene, Kansas, for Mom to do his laundry? (Years later I would hear of the Rubber Barons in Manaus, Brazil, shipping their laundry to Europe!) I hope not. But this was my laundry box. Each week on a Friday afternoon, or possibly Saturday morning, I trekked up the hill from the dorm to Troost Avenue and up the street to a Laundromat. There all the washing and drying was done, and clothes were neatly folded for the return trip to the dorm. And that was that. The idea that the box was used twenty years earlier in Omaha, Nebraska, is indeed a bit curious.

Mark J. Curran

3. A Change of Major and a Goodbye to Science and Advanced Math

Dean Joseph Gough, S. J., Rockhurst College, 1963

So we settled in. Before I could buy books, a small but life changing matter had to be taken care of, and it involved my first encounter with a stern Jesuit. It's a bit foggy now, but after studying the class schedule and the required courses for the Liberal Arts Major which was my initial listing, it soon became apparent that I was headed for trouble. A major dose of advanced mathematics, probably algebra or calculus, and lab science, perhaps Biology, were required. I recall talking to one of the students from southern Missouri, a proclaimed pre-med person and looking at his biology text. Whoa. It was known that you could at least discuss this with a school official, in this case the old college Dean. Not any Dean, this was a dyed in the wool, you-can't-put-anything-over-on-me veteran, one Father Gough. I recall a fairly short person, black robe, white collar, grey hair; he was an altogether serious fellow. I stammered by case and pleaded to be switched from Liberal Arts to Business Management (I had gotten a few tips from boys in similar straits), saying I wanted to be

8

a businessman in Latin America, Spanish being my main interest. It was just as well there was no major in Spanish at Rockhurst because it would have been in Liberal Arts and I would have been tossed back into the math and science arena. Amazingly enough, Fr. Gough agreed to the change, and I ended up studying for a bachelor degree in Business Management with a minor in Spanish. The closest thing I came to math and science was a ridiculously easy Business Math Course I'll tell of later.

In retrospect it's the consequences of that conversation that count, one of those decisions, days, and events that in reality change your whole life. I am sure I would have flunked out of Rockhurst if I had to do the math and science. On the other hand, the change brought eventual academic success, a national NDEA Fellowship for a Ph.D., a career as a university teacher and researcher and writer of many books. In addition, it instilled in me, first of all, a grateful attitude to that Jesuit (I believe after some study he indeed deviated from the "Ratio Studiorum") but more important, a tolerance in my later teaching career in language and culture classes for those students enrolled strictly because of a university language requirement and who have no gift for language at all. Right or wrong, I have told them: Come to class, make a solid effort, do the work, and we'll see how it turns out. They got the benefit of the doubt. Now did stern Father Gough think thusly in 1959? I do not know.

4. The Jesuit Experience

Before continuing with the day to day of that first year in college, there are some loose ends to tie down. From the outset, the students heard the school motto—"Sapientia Aedificavit Sibi Domum" ["Wisdom Hath Built Herself a Home"] and were expected to memorize it. The motto was on the school coat of arms and appeared to be emblazoned everywhere on campus. Equally important was the motto of the Jesuit Order itself: "Ad Majorem Dei Gloriam" ["To the Greater Glory of God"]. An aside (there will be many): Years after Rockhurst I would invoke the Jesuit saying as a sort of prayer before playing music on the classical guitar before Sunday mass at a little parish church in Colorado. And I did indeed dedicate the effort to the greater glory of God. It is doubtful that my melodious strains not helped by cold stiff fingers on the guitar strings at that hour of morning augmented God's glory, but I loved the prayer.

Mark, Classical Guitar, St. Bartholomew's Catholic Church, Bayfield, Colorado

The Jesuits believed that the student should receive aside from his academic major and minor interests a solid religious formation, thus there were if I am not mistaken 24 credit hours required in Theology and Philosophy. They were following the "Ratio Studiorum" instituted in 1599, with high hopes to develop virtue and wisdom in their college students. Latin, studies of Classic Literature, Physical Education and such from the old days were followed in college by emphasis on Theology and Philosophy. In my case these courses were exactly that—requirements—and held little interest for me. Theology at first was a study of the four Gospels and lit no fire in me. Philosophy was much more difficult, quite abstract at times, and also did not either inspire or take me to intellectual heights. Courses like Philosophy of Being and Ethics I barely passed; they were very difficult and not my cup of tea. Only one course, History of Philosophy, sparked a modicum of interest.

What really would have made an impression on me, although I am writing this from a perspective of today in 2010 at a much older age in retirement, would have been a solid and dynamic course on the founding of the Jesuits, the struggles to begin the Order and to be recognized as such by the Pope, the early efforts in Paris and then Rome, in hospitals and schools, and especially the missionary efforts of the followers of Ignacio de Loyola and Francisco Xavier to India, Japan, China, and to my area of interest, Latin America. You could have called it "History of the Jesuit Order, 101." I would learn much of this later on in adulthood sparked by an unintended visit to Loyola in northern Spain's Basque Country, the home of Ignacio de Loyola. These were great men of a singular inspiring mission in life, and they truly were discoverers, colonists and heroes. I only learned later of the role of the Jesuits at the Council of Trent defending the Roman Catholic Church and the role of faith and action in the movement to defend the church against the Protestant Reformation, in effect, beginning the Counter-Reformation in Spain. Some of this I did learn through reading and classes in Spanish Literature at Saint Louis University later on. But nothing of the sort seemed to be in the curriculum at Rockhurst in 1959. I add that later on the romanticized adventure film in the 1970s "The Mission," with Robert de Niro and Jeremy Irons would certainly buttress my idealized vision of the Jesuit Missionaries. I plugged the film for years at Arizona State and all the Mormon Missionaries (RMs they were called) shared the spirit of it all.

The Jesuits indeed had their "system" worked out through 400 years of high school and college educational experience. As mentioned before, there is a Latin term for it, the "Ratio Studiorum." It is the plan for their college curriculum. You figure they must have known what would work. I can simply say this: with one or two large exceptions, and both in graduate school, (much will be said about those two Jesuits later), it was the lay teacher or teachers at Rockhurst and later on at Saint Louis University who inspired me and would encourage me to greater things in the future. I refer to my undergraduate Spanish professor Mr. Vernon Long and to Professors Edward Sarmiento and Doris Turner later on at Saint Louis. Of course, it was the Jesuits who discovered and hired such teachers.

I think it all boils down to the difference between undergraduate and graduate school. At Rockhurst we were young, we were trying to figure out the most basic interests in life and we probably needed some "shepherding." At Saint Louis it was an entirely different matter; there was a specific goal and a way to get there. The Jesuits at Rockhurst were teaching required courses and not the kind of thing most young men would or could sink their teeth in to, i.e. Theology, Philosophy.

At Saint Louis I would be studying subjects and subject matter that truly inspired me and would become a life-long pursuit. So in view of this and those courses, the Jesuits, yes, were inspiring at Saint Louis University. Foremost were Father Rosario Mazza, director of the Modern Language Department and professor of Spanish, one of several priests from Trinidad, Colorado, near Pueblo and the steel factory and obviously children of the Italian immigrants there, and Father John Bannon, a renowned historian of the U.S. Southwest and Latin America. There will be much more about this in Part III.

Credit should be given, however, to those Rockhurst Jesuits who made stalwart efforts to teach us of our faith, introduce us to critical thinking and hopefully enthuse us with the heroes of our faith tradition. They faced a sometimes insurmountable obstacle: the immaturity of the 19 year old.

Having expressed a bit of the pro and con in a very initial stage of Jesuit education, my goal in this portion of the text is to tell of the total experience, perhaps recalling for the reader what it used to be like to be with the Jesuits in school in the 1960s.

The Annual Retreat

Among the Jesuit traditions that they did follow at Rockhurst was the once-a-year retreat, mandatory at that. I believe that I went through one each year, but memories are hazy. I am sure, now, that they were based on Ignacio de Loyola's Spiritual Exercises. I think it was my first one freshman year that made the biggest impression; it was indeed a powerful experience. What I recall were many talks, beginning Friday night, time for meditation, a major examination of conscience and confession, and more talks and mass through Sunday noon. I recall I returned to the dorm totally exhausted but feeling wonderful and a bit holy. I cannot recall the content of the talks, but remember that they were quite dramatic, the Jesuit in his black robe, candles and their illumination, and I think a fair amount of fire and brimstone. The idea of course was to cleanse oneself of past sins, be united with Christ with a clean slate and communion. The confession was what we might have called a general confession delving back to earliest memories, sins and confessing them all. (At age seventy as I write this I can only chuckle at the "serious" sins a nineteen year old could have related during the retreat.) I have not made one such confession since. It was indeed cleansing and exhausting. Too bad we young college guys with raging hormones would soon sin again. Most people were not lucky (or unlucky) enough to have to confess real sex with one of the local Catholic school girls. I must say that the annual retreat was probably one of the Jesuits' strongest traditions that we did experience at Rockhurst.

Weekly Mass and the "Cut" System

Another "tradition" was Jesuit discipline and the cut system for classes; you were allowed one cut per credit hour of class during the entire semester, i.e. 3 hr. class, 3 cuts. There was a hitch: if you missed the required mass at St. Francis Xavier College Church on Friday, it was a triple cut, and if you missed class before and after a holiday, another triple cut. The system was applied vigorously, but the exact bookkeeping is still a mystery to me. We students watched the numbers and I don't recall getting into trouble about it. Years later during my early years as a professor at Arizona State University when I tried to apply a similar "cut" system, my supervisor and chair called me in and said, "Mark, you have to remember you are now at a public university and not a Jesuit school."

There was also a sort of very personal discipline early on at Rockhurst and it served me well: after each class I typed the hand written class notes on my Smith-Corona. It helped to rethink what had been said in class, organize thoughts a bit and preserve the information for the inevitable tests to come. One time freshman year a buddy down the hall in the dorm, John Tobin, wanted my notes from Theology class. I said no and he bopped me one.

This narrative will be replete with good times in these undergraduate days, but with a disclaimer: the Jesuits required a study hall each night in the dorms, I think from Sunday through Thursday and at least for the first two years. What I can add is that basically from Sunday night, or even Sunday afternoon through the end of classes on Friday, it was classes and study. And often there was work to be done on Saturday afternoon as well. Yet Friday and Saturday nights were left to blow off steam and have fun, and we did. In my case the grade point average was slowly built through the first years and maintained in the upper division with eventual graduation with honors; it was a combination of Jesuit and personal discipline.

5.   The First Day of Classes

The day of the first class arrived and turned out to be a really traumatic event for me. I had looked at my class schedule and checked out all the class rooms in Massman Hall prior to that day, but for some reason at the last moment I got confused. All this led to a very embarrassing moment and some resentment yet today. The class was European Civilization, a history course I was really excited about, having heard good things of the professor, one Father Huger. I arrived late to the class, perhaps by five minutes, can't recall if I knocked on the door, but hurriedly entered the room and took a chair at one of the desks remaining in the front row. The priest asked who I was, where I had been, and was obviously irritated at the interruption in this the first lecture of the term. Dressed in the standard black robe, belt, white, priestly collar and with a serious demeanor, this was Father Huger. Now for some reason, I had a pink, can you believe it, pink sweater on. Huger never forgot; from then on he would suddenly point a finger in my direction and say, "Mr. Curran, you of the pink sweater, what did the Romans have to do with Gaul?" Or some such question. On the surface I took it as a joke; it was out of the question to ask him please to forget the pink sweater. I never missed a single class, took copious notes, and earned a B in the final, no small accomplishment. I recall the exams were multiple-choice, but incredibly well prepared, tricky and difficult. I probably have forgotten much of the subject matter, but never the priest. He evidently had done some teaching or mission work in India, and we made fun of him with his oft repeated statement, "When I was in Indiaaa" . . . pronouncing the last word like a veteran of the old British East India Company. I never forgot that first day. Today I believe his actions were totally uncalled for, a real bullying of a young, naïve, beginning student. Thus was the beginning of my education under the Jesuits. Some might have packed their bags.

The unfortunate pink sweater does jog the memory about our dress for classes. We wore slacks, neat shirts or a sweater; I do not believe we normally wore coat and tie, but there were times we did. But certainly there were no blue jeans and t-shirts from high school days.

6.   Better Days in Other Classes

A much more pleasant but demanding experience was my introduction to college level Spanish. Because of the two years at Abilene High School with the dedicated schoolmarm Miss Edberg, I was placed in SPA 201, intermediate. The teacher was highly qualified and even more motivated. He would not only teach me, but mentor me and encourage me to do greater things. Mr. Vernon Long of New Orleans, Louisiana, with an M.A. from Louisiana State U. in Baton Rouge, was equally proficient in Spanish and French. The class was full to capacity with twenty-plus students, and there were at least a handful of students who were more advanced than I, particularly one or two who not only knew grammar but could rattle off nice oral Spanish. My preparation in structure, grammar, and culture at Abilene High School was excellent, but I was not taught nor did I have much speaking proficiency. So that first day when EVERYTHING was in Spanish was scary. This was something I wanted to do badly, so I hung in there and soon was near the top of the class.

An aside, but something important that sticks with me today: Professor Long's Spanish was clear, crisp, correct and fluent. This became my lifelong model and pleasure; years later both in Spanish and Brazilian Portuguese, in dealings with native speakers in the U.S. and in Latin America my day was made when I could speak to natives with . . . clear, crisp and well enunciated Spanish or Portuguese. Years later at Arizona State, the native speakers from Spain and Latin America would say that Curran, although not a native speaker, was the absolute best role model possible for Anglo Americans who wanted to learn Spanish, that my Spanish was both correct and well pronounced, even if not "quite" native. Hey, I'll take that yet today.

So through the four years at Rockhurst I would work through the progression in Spanish: intermediate, composition and conversation, Peninsular Literature and Introduction to Spanish American Literature. I think I had straight A's and a love for the language and culture that would take me far. Certainly Vernon Long was the professor that inspired me most and mentored me best at Rockhurst.

7. Learning Spanish Outside of Class

There was more. I searched out and made my first friends from Latin America, the first a fellow from Chihuahua, Mexico, and then an Ecuadorean from Quito. With the latter, we spoke Spanish while I "took him to school" in pool games in the dorm basement where I parted him from some U.S. dollars. Later on, sophomore through senior years, one of my best and lasting friendships from Latin America was with Eduardo Matheu from Guatemala. I will have much more to say about him and our adventures later on. So it was: it was outside of class that I really tried to figure out ways and times to actually speak Spanish. It came slowly, but surely. Yet today I counsel my students: there are two paths to proficiency and both are necessary—classroom preparation with structure and practice and oral practice in some fashion with native speakers.

8. Expenses and Jobs

Dad and Mom paid my major expenses at Rockhurst, at least until junior or senior year when my grades would garner a tuition scholarship. I am sure Dad borrowed much of this money and prayed and waited on good crops to pay off the loans. I always prided myself on having three jobs while in school, one in particular I am not very proud of today. A silver tongued, street-wise and clever upper classman, Steve Prenger, singled me out to take over the Ligget and Myer Cigarette distribution program in the dorm. For $25 a month and all the cigarettes I could smoke, I would receive huge boxes of L & Ms, Oasis and Chesterfield cigarettes each month. My job was to give them away to any takers. After a while no one would even take them, and the boxes stacked up in the dorm room. I am fairly certain this job lasted only one year, a good thing. What remained was the habit of smoking and knowing now I indirectly contributed to the habits of others. We heard no news of smoking and cancer then, but that does not make me feel any better. An aside—I gave out entire packs of cigarettes, perhaps with 30 cigarettes, but these were the times when all airline passengers would receive a pack of 4 cigarettes, gratis, on all the flights. So I wasn't the only one hustling.

The Continental All-Stars Dance Band, Rockhurst College, 1960

The second job as a language laboratory assistant was given to me by Professor Long. It involved putting on language tapes for students, rewinding them and keeping them in the proper library spots. I think I also actually collected homework papers for the teachers. The main memory was that the lab was good for its times, and that the tapes were reel to reel, played on the old Wollensok recorders. It's hard to believe but they were still in use at Arizona State in 1968 even though ASU had a very advanced language lab to service perhaps a dozen languages. Once I hauled an old Wollensok to Portuguese classes to play Brazilian pop music to inspire the kids. They were inspired but howled at my old recorder, for now the small cassette tape machines were in vogue and at the end CDs as well. Hours were spent at Arizona State by the lab director and his assistant playing my original 33 rpm disk LPs and converting them first to reel to reel and then to cassettes.

That brings me to a third "job," not really a job but an activity that would bring in a few shekels later on, very few. I would play in two bands at Rockhurst. The first may have brought in a few bucks, but not enough for me to remember today. This was my first and only experience with what we used to call "dance bands." The band was organized by one of the few Jewish boys I ever met, Charles . . . from Chicago. Charles was steeped in big band tradition and wanted a version of it for Rockhurst. I mainly recall him as being very . . . demanding. He was "da boss," however. Anyway, he found these cardboard music stands; we put our chairs behind them, and away we went. Our group was called "The Continental All Stars." Charles played trumpet; we had trombone from a very humorous guy from a small town in northern Missouri, a couple of saxophones, maybe a clarinet, piano, drums and my "sort of" rhythm guitar, a Kay electric with small amplifier. We practiced once a week in one of the empty classrooms, and the tunes were the "old standards," many I guess from the 30s, 40s, and 50s, including Glen Miller pieces. The pianist, good friend Bill Bockelman from St. Louis, had a "fake" book, so he could do about any melody. The drummer was that one-night roommate from Gallup, Phil Kezele. There were all these funny twists: you always had to have at least one "solo" by the drummer, just those pounding drums inspired I think by Gene Krupa. I don't know if the guitar ever merited any solos, mainly because I did not know many, but I think I did the lead on "Honky Tonk," an early rock tune of the times, maybe from Duane Eddy's "Twangy" guitar. Everyone got their time in the limelight, merited or not. I can't remember how often we played, but the above illustration is from playing a dance at Rockhurst in the old Rock Room in Massman Hall. I think it all ended when Charlie graduated since he was a year or two ahead of me. We would wear sport coat and tie, maybe a dark blue Rockhurst blazer, which coincidentally I was told to purchase freshman year for debate team.

9.   Debate at Rockhurst

During this first year at Rockhurst I was motivated to continue an activity I had excelled in at Abilene High School—Debate (we won the state championship when I was a senior.) Such an effort resulted in my altogether too brief time spent on Rockhurst's debate team. My partner's name was Tom Grosbeak from Saint Louis University High Prep School. He was an upper classman and very, very intelligent. Steve Prenger, he of the silver tongue of free cigarette fame was also on the team. There was very limited time to prepare in comparison to Abilene High School days where debate team was first priority. Class preparation and exams simply had to take priority at Rockhurst. I did debate in two or three tournaments and only recall the last one, at Wichita State University. My partner and I drew Harvard! This is like Rockhurst's NAIA basketball squad playing the Boston Celtics. Funny, at the tournament in Wichita I recall sitting at the desk with my partner Tom and into the room walk these two slick "suits" from Harvard U. They carried huge briefcases, supposedly containing file boxes with all their proofs and such stuff and not just their lunch. They handed us OUR lunch soon enough; all I recall were very crisp, well-prepared speeches. The contest did not exactly take the turn of the recent movie with Denzel Washington, "The Great Debaters," when Washington's minority students whipped Harvard's ass in the film. We returned meekly to Rockhurst, not exactly with tail between the legs, but a bit chagrined by it all at the time. However, it makes for a nice little anecdote from those days. I had to move on to other things.

10. Big Town, Small Town, Jesuit Prep Schools and Small Town Public High School, the Social Situation

It is important to tell of the "social" situation at Rockhurst which inevitably brings me to talk of what I perceived then of "Jesuit Prep School" cliques and maybe some big city prejudice, perhaps a tad unwarranted, toward the small town boys from Kansas, Missouri and a few thrown in from Iowa or Illinois. I can remember being kidded, perhaps not so good—naturedly, about being a country boy from Abilene, a Republican at that, and some jokes about what us farm boys supposedly were doing with the animals on the farm. Not understanding this "allusion" until perhaps an Ethics course and the mention of the word "bestiality," I guess we indeed missed out on a part of Western Civilization in Abilene. The joking of course did not endear me to the "big city" boys, most of them prep school graduates from Rockhurst and Saint Louis University high schools. It is perfectly natural that they would maintain old friendships and habits, and to their credit a half dozen or so seemed friendly enough. But common backgrounds and interests attract. So it was that my best friends were to become my roommate from small-town Concordia in Kansas, Jim Fitzgerald, Paul Steichen from Salina, Kansas, Jim Maloney from a farm outside Junction City, John Tobin from the quad city area in Illinois, and especially Bill Rost from Jefferson City, Missouri, my partner in crime in the hillbilly radio program we did for the annual Rockhurst Variety Show. Exceptions to the cliques were Bill Bockelman from SLU High and partner in the dance band and Denny Noonan from St. Louis, but not SLU High. Tim Braithwaite was another, but from a non-Jesuit high school in Kansas City.

Friendships with Latin Americans would become paramount for me, keeping in mind the interest and future goal of a career using Spanish and later on, Portuguese, thinking in particular of Eduaro Matheu from Guatemala and Henrique Kerti from Brazil. What is of interest is that my Anglo friends voted me "Most outstanding Latino Student" senior year. There were slight friendships with some of the prep school guys. Arnold Dill of SLU High did me a huge favor, perhaps not realizing it, directing me to my first classic guitar concert; Tom Sarsfield who was always friendly, and a few others. Perhaps I protest too much.

Social life with all these guys on campus was really fine and normal "college stuff:" shooting the breeze with buddies in the dormitory, conversation over coffee and cigarettes in the student union's Rock Room before, between and after classes, and a lot of great conversation in the cafeteria at the evening meal time. I repeat that one specific occasion marks the time: we were all sitting in the Rockhurst cafeteria after the evening meal listening to the news on the Cuban Missile Crisis—the discovery by our spy plane of Soviet long-range nuclear missiles in Cuba and the ensuing negotiations, demands and threats by Krushchev and John F. Kennedy's answer. We were sure that night we would all be drafted into the service for a war to come.

11. Did You Say "Girls?"

Freshman year was also marked by that famous Catholic boys/girls college institution: the mixer. I can recall yet bumming a ride over to St. Teresa's College and standing around at the dance too shy or nervous to ask any chicks to dance. Eventually I did meet one cute gal, a graduate of Bishop Miege High School on the Kansas side, and did date her for a while. Nothing came of it, probably a mutual decision. I did appreciate her sweetness and by the way her well-developed physique. And there were mixers on campus at Rockhurst in the Rock room with either a DJ playing pop music of the times or perhaps a band of some sort. We dressed in white shirt, tie, slacks and sport coat for the occasion. Then those of us without automobiles, i.e. dates, took our horny selves back to the dorm afterwards.

Things would change junior year when I finally would have a car on campus; in fact things changed a lot. My old car, the 1953 salmon colored Dodge with "gyro-torque," (a term for a "slushomatic" transmission in those days) lovingly called "The Pink Tit," was the main transportation. I am amazed today when I think of those days and how I drove freely about greater Kansas City and home to Abilene in that old wreck. With a car you could actually ask a girl out and if she liked you and your car enough there might have been a second date. It must have worked because later on during senior year roommate Tim Braithwaite's girl Kathy would set me up on a blind date with her girlfriend Ellen, and she became my companion for a few dates.

12. College Boy Returns Home for the First Time

I can honestly say that homesickness was not a major issue that first year away from home. Not that I did not think of home. There was a ritual letter each week home to Mom and Dad and I looked forward to their letters as well. Mail call was really an anticipated time! The first trip home was at Thanksgiving, and I probably was guilty of the syndrome of now being a "big man on campus" home to see the old small town and friends. I would hitch rides with my brother Jim who was now living in a boarding house on the Missouri side and was working for a passenger elevator manufacturing company. My strongest memory of those rides back and forth to Abilene was the incredibly smoky car; Jim chain smoking and I guess I was puffing by then too. It was a miracle my parents did not get cancer from secondary smoke since Jim filled the house with it for at least twenty years. The family celebrated Thanksgiving and I probably went up to the Duffy bowling alley in Abilene in search of a glimpse of the old high school flame, Mary Ann. But I think by this time she was well on to a different phase of life and boyfriends.

A more memorable trip home was during Christmas vacation that freshman year. The event was a penny-ante poker game at Jim Forren's mother's house on Rogers, the same street where my parents would live after Dad sold the farm a few years later. High school buddies Jim Forren, Jerry Hawks I think, Kenny Klufa, Mike Kippenberger, myself, and perhaps Ron Gardner as well made up the poker table. A good, innocent time was had by all, swapping stories I am sure of what it was like to be in college. But we drank a lot of beer too. I must have still been living out on the farm, because I think Mike was driving and was going to give me a ride home. Anyway, we were cruising towards Mike's house on the east side of town and ended up in the neighborhood where our former high school principal lived. Somehow or other we drove up over the curb well into his manicured yard, almost hitting the house. Details and dialogue are a bit fuzzy, but the gist of the discussion going on in what seemed like those dreams where everything is super slowed down, was, "What the shit! What do you think? Let's take off!" So we drove off the other side of the lawn and were heading up Brady Street toward Mike's house when the red-blue police car lights came on. Some cop had seen the whole thing. They hauled us down to the police station and eventually called Mike's Dad to come down and take us home. No charges were filed, a big difference from what would probably happen today. A singular memory was sitting on a wooden bench in the police station and being very preoccupied about my muddy shoes, peeling off the mud, rolling it into little balls and tossing it into the waste basket in the corner. We of course were punished more by the silent treatment; Joe Kippenberger did not raise his voice, but we were basically told to "straighten up." I'm sure Christmas was fine, gifts under the tree, Midnight Mass and great food from Mom's kitchen, but the Poker Party Incident only happened once.

There was one other event when I came home to visit; it must have been a year or two later because Mom and Dad were now living in town. I related it in "The Farm." Dad kept horses for himself and kids from town out at a barn in a lot at the northeast corner of the old farm. They were turned loose, we suspect as a prank by some local beer drinking teenagers. It was one of those freezing nights in winter with temperatures hovering around zero, and Mom, Dad and I spend a good while corralling the horses thus keeping them from getting through or over a fence out onto the Interstate. The small Kansas farm met Progress head on that night.

13. From Freezing Winter to Freezing Summer— Abilene and the Ice Plant

The summer after frosh year I returned to Abilene where I worked long hours at the local ice plant. It's worthwhile to tell some of the story. The ice plant was the old fashioned kind and had been around for at least fifty or sixty years. It was owned by Paul Huffman, a friend of my Dad's, I think through the Elks. Anyway, I was offered a full-time summer job, perhaps starting at $1.15 per hour. I had lots of overtime and worked up to 60 hours per week, including Saturdays. The ice plant was located south of the Union Pacific tracks in a complex of buildings that used to be a hotel, called a drovers' cottage in the old days for cowboys coming up the Chisholm Trail from Texas on the cattle drives which ended in Abilene. Among many claims to fame, the ice house employed no less than Dwight D. Eisenhower as a young man.

The ice was made the old fashioned way: tanks with fresh water were dunked into the salt brine to freeze, later hoisted out on pulleys, the tanks were turned on their sides and the cakes of ice fell out and slid to the ice house. The 300 pound cakes of ice, standing vertically, were scored into sections, five on each side, of 30 pounds. We would take ice picks and split the cake into thirty pound blocks and either push them to a conveyor belt for sale to the public at a vending machine outside the ice house facing the street, or put them in an ice crusher where the 30 pounds were put in paper bags for crushed ice for the same retail consumer.

One of my main jobs was to run the local "ice route" in an old pickup truck, a 1954 orange Chevy. Stacked in the back were many bags of crushed ice I would deliver to drug stores and the like, but also a few cakes of ice I would split into 60 and 30 pound blocks to be distributed to a few old-fashioned customers. Among the latter was the bakery. I would park in the back alley, carry the blocks (I had trouble lifting the 60 pound blocks, but would split them into two 30s), tote them down a rickety, narrow stairway to the basement and put in the old bakery icebox. I was rewarded with cookies and other fineries of the bakery. There was only one residential customer, a little old lady on Sixth Street who would put the "ice" sign in her window, and I would carry perhaps 60 pounds into her old icebox. One memory remains: one day with two or three cakes of ice still in the back of the pickup which had an iron chain across the back to hold it all in, I came to the Union Pacific Tracks, pulled out a little too fast, and all that ice was dumped out onto the street of South Buckeye, the main north-south street in Abilene. I stopped, and stopped traffic, picked up what I could and the rest was left to melt in the street. Don't know if Mr. Huffman's profits suffered much from that at all.

As an added source of income at the plant, extra cold storage rooms were kept for ice cream from one of the retailers in the area; and watermelons and such were also stored there. One of our duties was to unload the ice cream truck and store the gallon containers in the storage room. We managed to accidentally throw a gallon or two over the chicken wire fence separating that storage room from another at the ice plant. The end of the story is that we had watermelon, ice cream and other goodies to munch on a time or two.

It was at the ice plant that I really began to have a chance to practice my infant Spanish. There were two fine local Hispanics who worked there; we became friends and evidently because of my sincerity in this task, I was invited to their home for dinner. This was the first time I had actually tasted real Mexican food: the family fixed me a treat, "mole poblano," probably the spiciest of all Mexican foods. It was a far cry from the fried chicken and mashed potatoes on the farm. I managed to get though the meal, enjoyed the hospitality but paid the consequences the next day. I did speak a lot of rudimentary Spanish with those hard-working Mexicans in Abilene. And we laughed a lot.

Nighttimes in that summer and perhaps two more were spent at Howie's Tavern on Third Street, an altogether pleasant experience when I could spend one dollar on ten cent draft beers and have a nice evening. It was then I had many talks with Bill Jeffcoat the local photographer and listened with great attention to his tales of photographing the local visits of Dwight D. Eisenhower to Abilene. He chronicled those times and eventually did a book on Eisenhower. But often on those hot summer nights high school buddies, Bob Hensley, a fine bongo player, Eddy Smith and his guitar, and me with mine would venture out to Eisenhower Park to the band shell and play pop, country and folk music, and a good time was had by all. For romance I dated a local girl and we spent many nights at the drive-in movie in Salina and the hormones were strong. A good Catholic background and fear of the fires of hell kept me out of any more serious trouble. Not that I was not tempted. I don't know which films we saw, but we had a good time.

That is how I passed the summer between freshman and sophomore year at Rockhurst, and perhaps another summer later on as well.

B. SOPHOMORE YEAR AT ROCKHURST

I returned to Rockhurst and the Jesuits in the fall. There was work in the language laboratory as an assistant, and my mentor Vernon Long now introduced me to Spanish Literature and Culture. It all went well, and the Spanish was progressing. This was the most important development that year.

1. Basketball Games, Cheering on the Team and the End of a Singing Voice

Rockhurst was then an NAIA sports team. We dorm students never missed a home basketball game, sitting on the front row of the tiny gymnasium cheering on the team. It was at this time that from the intense cheering and spurring on the team yelling at the top of my lungs so many nights I did some real damage to my vocal chords. I can only remember vaguely the visit to the throat specialist, sore throat and all, and the consequences. I cannot explain the physical part of this, but I am sure than the damage done to my vocal chords caused me to lose the ability to do a falsetto effect. What I mean is the ability to skip to another octave in singing, much as John Denver always did in his songs. Country singers and yodelers do it all the time. Since I was not to become anything close to a truly professional singer, this had no great consequences, but it did have minor ones: in later years I could not do that jump in octave when I tried to sing "El Paso" by Marty Robbins or such stuff.

However, the basketball team did well and it was great fun. My senior year they placed 2nd in the NAIA, and the next year won it all. I still remember the hot shot outside shooter and a relatively small, for now, guard named Ralph Telken who would race down the court and dunk it! I understand he took his artistic talents after graduation to Hallmark Cards in Kansas City, designing such things. This was well before the time of the big boppers and dunkers in college basketball. The only such one I recall was Luke Jackson of Pan American from Texas, a tall black athlete about 6 foot six who was ahead of his time. The gym was really quite tiny, but the cheerleaders were enthusiastic, the crowds filled the small place and it was fun basketball. Would I trade these memories for the better voice? Yes.

In the spring we would watch the Rockhurst baseball team now and again. It was pretty "small" stuff with the team playing on a field just north of the dormitory; there was not even a stadium of sorts. There are few memories, but I loved baseball. One memory was that of Tom Sarsfield, a stalwart from St. Louis University High School who was a fine pitcher and all-around athlete. Tom, who, by the way, was always friendly to me, the small town guy, was a sight to see, either pitching or hitting a home run. I understand that Rockhurst has upgraded the baseball facility since those years, a little late for me, but a good thing.

2. Academics, Classes, Jesuits and Others

DIVISION OF PHILOSOPHY AND THEOLOGY STANDING: Left to Right, Aloysius M. Rieckus, S. J., Theology; Jules M. Brady, S. J., Philosophy; Robert J. Kreyche, Philosophy; SEATED: Charles A. Nash, Theology; Edward J. Ziegelmeyer, S. J., Philosophy; John J. O'Brien, S. J., Philosophy; Robert J. VandenBurgt, Philosophy Chairman William L. Rossner, Philosophy; Justin X. Schmitt, S. Philosophy; Samuel J. Kennedy, Philosophy; Joseph M. Freeman S. J., Philosophy, and Vincent F. Daues, S. J., Theology.

The Jesuits, Theology and Philosophy, Rockhurst College

At some point in all this I need to talk about classes, the Jesuit professors and their personalities. The courses they taught comprised the required minors in Theology and Philosophy and were all on the undergraduate level. We students were all so young and immature, and I was just one of the crowd taking the required courses. Still, their presence is part of this story of what I believe was a "typical" Jesuit undergraduate experience in the late 1950s and early 1960s.

Theology was required, and one of the few courses I recall was just that, the required "Theology 101" taught by one Father Justin Schmidt, S. J., a tall and actually very handsome Jesuit in his customary black robe and white collar. The main subject matter was to be a "careful" reading of the four Gospels of the New Testament. I did this, but without too much enthusiasm, probably garnering an A or a B in the course. Understanding what was in those readings fifty years later seems more important. I will read the Bible yet today, most likely when times are a bit challenging.

A second Jesuit-taught course would be one of the philosophy courses, and in fact we were required to have a minor in Philosophy by the time we graduated, 6 courses for 18 credit hours. Since I found it very abstract and difficult, I simply fulfilled the requirement. For Rockhurst associated readers of this narrative, I'll jot down a few memories.

There was Father Brady who taught Philosophy of Being. He was a good lecturer, mainly by virtue that he had written the textbook. But there was a catch—to us, he seemed to have it memorized and the daily lecture followed the book verbatim. When the final class bell rang he stopped and it seemed like the next day began with the same sentence. Or so we thought. For us, this became the epitome of the then used term, the "canned" lecture. I should not have cast the first stone; I'm sure I memorized a part of his text to try to pass the exams. I may have made a B.

Father Rossner was an extremely distinguished gentleman who taught one of the advanced courses, Ethics I think. He was one of the senior professors of the Philosophy section. He was truly versed in Philosophy and as I vaguely recall could bring in all the heavy hitters—Socrates, Aristotle and on up to Thomas Aquinas, whose famous "Summa Theologica" was required reading. We of course all made fun of the questions such as "How many angels could fit on the head of a pin?" Little of Father Rossner's wisdom rubbed off on me through no fault of his own. I might have made a B.

My favorite was Father Ziegelmeyer who taught History of Philosophy. Quite elderly at the time, perhaps senior Jesuit statesman on campus, this priest was always prone to humor, a big smile, and bursts of laughter. He took us through the rudiments of ancient Greek philosophy. One truism of undergraduate life is "Which books did you keep?" That book was one of the few in Philosophy I kept after graduation. The course was an easy A and one bit of wisdom he passed on, in veiled language related to sex, was "It gets easier when you get older." Not soon enough for most of us! I suspect he was in his upper 70s or even early 80s.

By far the most difficult of the Jesuits was the man I unluckily drew for Freshman English, Father Price. He was good and he was serious. There were many texts required for the course; the one I remember most was "The Dialogues of Plato" which we read, discussed (although not much by me) and were asked to write something intelligent about on essay exams from hell. For whatever reason, I was grateful and uncomplaining to garner a C in this class. The returned assignments and term papers were filled with red ink, and I did not seem to have much insight into Plato. Oh well.

An aside is in order. I just read recently, once again, one of my favorite Brazilian writers, Luís Fernando Veríssimo, one of Brazil's great humorists and a writer of short prose pieces called "chronicles." One I just read on the bus to ASU was "Grammar," and his sentiments fit mine exactly—the main point is to write "clearly" and the rest is, well, grammar.

Other Jesuits come to mind; several of whom I did not actually have for class were renowned about campus. Father Diebold was the English professor for the "buttheads," and I should have been amongst them. He swore like a drunken sailor in class, the F bomb among the splendid use of that sort of lexicon. He was very human, understood the 20 year old red blooded boys' needs and regaled them with fine stories. It was also gossiped about he enjoyed the scotch and other evening libations up at the Jesuit residence. How do I know? I don't, but friends from his classes related these details. There was a bit of local "folklore" about the fine food, the libations and such at the Jesuit residence at Rockhurst. Like folklore, it is just that. A scene from the recent Hollywood movie "Doubt" comes to mind when the problematic priest and his crony priests and the bishop dine on filet mignon and fine wine with scotch highballs (it is supposed) on the table. The school nuns do penance on water and simple food at the other end of the school complex.

Father Lakas was another English professor I did not have, probably a pity. He was a bit of a dandy, immaculately dressed in the black robes and upon occasion in black suit, shoes and priestly collar, waiting to be picked up in the big black Cadillac by the wife of a rich donor to the school. It was understood that he was serving as her academic escort, perhaps confessor, and partner at the local opera in Kansas City. The donating family was famous in the city with Cadillac dealerships I believe, and I surmise Father Lakas was instrumental in some of the donations. He was fine in the classroom, so I heard, especially in matters of literature and high culture.

The Jesuits sponsored other cultural high points during the year. Rockhurst had a regular lyceum schedule, and there was a lecture with Robert Frost the poet and yet another with Samuel Eliot Morrison, the major historian in the U.S. on naval history.

Then, there was the feisty Jesuit feared by all, Father Freeman, who lived into his nineties and also taught Philosophy. I was not about to get near that man's course. He would come down to the dorm and roughhouse with those courageous enough to play in handball and basketball games.

There is one other priest to be mentioned, the only Jesuit I had for business courses. He taught economic theory, and I managed a low B in that course. The mathematical formulas and diagrams were a bit much for me. I have told the story many times to students at ASU: I would prop one arm up on the desk, placing my palm over my eyes and doze. I was positive he did not know. The idea of telling this anecdote at ASU of course was to impart to my students that I KNEW! Economic theory like my time in class at Rockhurst is hazy yet today. From the way the country is heading it may be just as hazy in Washington.

So those were the Kansas City Rockhurst Jesuits. Of course Father Van Ackeran, the college president and Father Gough, the aforementioned college dean, were always a presence, officiating at ceremonies and at mass. As I may have said, and it should be no surprise, one, because I never attended daily mass, two, because I was less than stellar in their courses, I was not approached or "recruited" for seminary as were a few stalwarts in the Philosophy and Theology classes, most from Jesuit prep schools as well. So be it.

So, one wonders, how in the devil did I garner an NDEA Fellowship to graduate school for a Ph.D. with the thus far mediocre and uninteresting academic performance? The answer is the list of A's garnered in a few business courses, majoring in Business Management, but mainly and above all the really fine record in four years of Spanish classes, ever increasing fluency garnered by actively searching out and making friendships with the Latino students at Rockhurst, and an entire summer dedicated seriously to the study of Spanish and Spanish Literature at the National University of Mexico in 1962. Allow me to tell some of the story.

3. Lay Teachers, My Formation

I've already told in some detail the encounter with Professor Vernon Long and the terrific experience in Spanish; as time passes, I'll come back to it.

DIVISION OF BUSINESS ADMINISTRATION LEFT TO RIGHT: B. J. ...enhawer, Accounting; James J. LePage, Management; Chairman ...yman F. Richter, Accounting; Edward M. Noonan, Marketing; Paul P. Rogers, Business Administration; Otis Miller, Business Administration.

The Business Faculty, Rockhurst College, early 1960s

I should talk of my major in Business Management and all that it involved; it is a curious story. I remind the reader that I became a business major for a very practical reason—not to do business, at least initially, but to avoid the math and science requirements of the Liberal Arts Major. Later on the business career did not seem to be such a bad idea. I need not recount the encounter with the Dean of the College who allowed me to make the switch to Business, but I want to talk a bit of the consequences. They have little to do with the Jesuits, except for the fact the Jesuit College Dean somehow, some way, approved my switch to Business Management before the first day of classes in 1959.

Let me start at the end: I graduated from Rockhurst with a very respectable grade point average for that time of 3.3 on a 4 point scale. A few of those A's came from the required business classes, but not many. Perhaps a short description will be of interest to anyone studying Business today and seeing the vast difference fifty years can make in the curriculum and the sophistication in business studies 50 years later. Many of the ASU students I taught over the years in Spanish or Portuguese were Business Management majors, or better yet, "Supply Stream Management."

The first memory of the business curriculum was the freshman class, Business Math. It was taught by an elderly gentleman, always dressed in suit and tie, with glasses and carrying his briefcase to class. The poor man was also a bit unaware. At Rockhurst in those days the professor lectured or conducted class with his chair and desk on a platform. The students would arrive early to class, balance the desk on the very edge of the platform, and he would walk in, put his briefcase on the table or lean on it and, blam! The whole thing would tumble over the edge onto the floor. Guffaws and heehawing would follow, or at least snickers by the more chagrined of us. I really felt sorry for the man. The tumbling table scene did happen two or three times during the semester. I cannot possibly conceive this happening in one of my classes later on as a professor. Another matter— everyone got the exams (as easy as business math could be)—and since everyone else had the tests, in self-defense you had to get them too. So this was the only instance in my college career that this happened. If the class average was 99, a respectable 80 would condemn you to a bad grade or maybe blow the cover for the cheats, most of them good upstanding Jesuit Prep School guys from Kansas City or St. Louis.

Rockhurst had some fine professionals among the business faculty, one a highly respected accountant with his own business in Kansas City, Missouri. I learned basic accountancy from him garnering a B or perhaps even an A. But there is a story here as well and how fate or destiny or ill winds have to do with far more than the "Iliad" or the "Odyssey" taught in freshman English class. The large part of the semester grade was based on the completion of a huge accounting problem, in effect, doing the yearly books for a fictitious company. It was nearly the end of the semester and I was working furiously on said project on a large table in the basement of the dorm where I could lay out all the papers. . . .

4.   Shenanigans and Some Good Luck

. . . up in a dormitory room, however, another drama would soon unfold. My buddy Paul Steichen and a couple of other students, and one other person, the son of the National Democratic Chairman, snuck a six pack (or more) of beer into the room and proceeded to have a bit of a party. They were caught red-handed and Jesuit disciplinary consequences were soon applied . . . more or less. Steichen, of a small town high school in Salina, Kansas, was summarily booted out of school. So was Paul Butler, the politician's son who sported in his dorm room no less than the podium banner for that year's National Democratic Convention when John F. Kennedy became the party's candidate for President of the United States. Butler, to be fair, also got the heave-ho. At that point, the denouement took place: Steichen transferred to a small business school in Salina, Kansas; Paul Butler, if my source is correct, was admitted to Notre Dame and as far as I know completed his illustrious college career at that august institution. Is it necessary to ask: Did Notre Dame know of the problem at Rockhurst? Did they care, after all, that the National Democratic Party Chairman's son was involved, and Kennedy was up and coming? And finally, were there any unofficial donations to grease the wheels in this academic transaction? All the above is conjecture and idle talk. Most importantly, there is another small matter: one could have Aristotelian certainty that had I not had the pressure of finishing the accounting problem, I would have been up in the dorm room swilling beer with the "delinquents." Thank you, Mr. Accounting Professor.

Did I tell of another prank of Steichen the denizen of the dormitory? On one occasion he ever so carefully took the tobacco out of a cigarette, clipped all his finger and toe nails, inserted them in the cigarette, filled in the tobacco and offered the smoke to a fellow who used to bum cigarettes constantly, but this time bummed one too many! Justice prevailed and vengeance of a sort was taken. The dormitory hall reeked with the smell when he lit up.

Steichen doubled us all over another time when he would lay on his back, pants off, fart and light the fart with a lighter. By now you may have guessed he was a bit fun-loving, and yet never experienced a painful anatomical blow up as far as I know.

5.   The Business Courses and the B.S.B.A.

Then there was the course in Marketing required for the Business Management majors. I remember just a bit of the course and the professor, Mr. Le Page, this time a young man who mistakenly confessed to his students that he was in the classroom because he could not withstand the pressures of the "real" business world. Red Flag! The term project is the point: one had to invent a product and work it through the standard marketing channels, one assumes from manufacture to retail store. It was here that a wiser Curran could have become a millionaire. My product was before its time: a classic, nylon-stringed guitar that could somehow be amplified. As far as I know in 1960 such a product did not exist on the market. But details or a few facts have never gotten in the way of finishing a term paper. I earned my B, got credit for the course and moved on another notch toward graduation. Note that every major guitar maker in its production factory today sports, and has for years, classic guitars with nylon stings which can be amplified and thus used for any venue beyond the quiet tiny classic concert hall.

A third example of the required business courses brings me to Mr. Noonan one of the senior professors for the major. I had perhaps two courses from him, the latter a general introduction to Business Law, a course taken during my last semester at Rockhurst. It was bandied about by the undergraduates that he had invested heavily in Brunswick Stock (the bowling alley industry) which had fallen upon hard times. My feelings have to be mixed as to this gentleman. I was with him in a senior course in actual analysis of business problems and earned an honest A. I would go on by virtue of my grades to actually receive honors in Business when graduating in 1963. But it is the final chapter of business studies at Rockhurst that involves Mr. Noonan — one of my last courses for the Business Management degree and graduation. I will relate that event come senior year.

6. Weather and the Seasons at Rockhurst

Another memory involves the seasons at Rockhurst, a minor point to be sure. But it is an important point for someone who has lived in the desert of Arizona for the last forty years. There were blooming flowers in spring, Kansas City heat and humidity in the summers, brilliant fall colors on the trees during that season, but I most recall days of cold and snow on the quadrangle. These were the days of trudging up the hill from the dormitory in snow or cold to get breakfast and attend the first class. The four seasons were very present in Kansas City. I shall tell in another spot of the blizzard and heavy snow and my guitar on a sled headed for a party with TWA stewardesses, all due to a connection with the Latinos and Eduardo Matheu.

7.   Underage Drinking and Friday Night Beer Blasts

Friday Night Beer Blast

To understand Rockhurst small college life, dormitory life, and being 19 years old in 1960, one has to talk about drinking and college life. At Rockhurst it was all a matter of legality: the drinking age in Missouri was 21; in Kansas for 3.2 beer only it was 18. Some students had phony I.Ds, but not yours truly. Too risky. So it was really a part of student life at the boys' school to organize the trek by taxi (no one was allowed cars freshman or sophomore year) a few miles to the Kansas side for swilling beer on Friday night. The debauchery took place on Friday because Saturday generally involved a dance at St. Teresa's girls' college or in the Rock Room on Rockhurst campus. There never seemed to be a lack of guys to be involved and split the hefty taxi fare. So Jim Fitzgerald, myself, maybe Paul Steichen, John Tobin, Jim Maloney and others would pile into the taxi and head to Kansas. The bar was called Sammy's and it was crowded and a good time was had by all. Really it was an innocent good time. The main beer was 3.2 Coors. I can recall the scene one night when the drunken St. Louis prep schoolers were saying "You can't get drunk on this 3.2 shit," while being, sorry, shit-faced. The times in that tavern were wonderful. There was great conversation, lots of singing of drinking songs, and finally, closing the bar and piling into a taxi to be poured into the rooms of the old dormitory on campus. I recall the decorations of the bar — that old scene of the dogs of all different breeds playing poker. In a way it was like a young boys' club. We were however introduced to a very real fact of life — terrific hangovers. If you thought to take a couple of aspirins before going to bed, it was a wise decision. But who would have thought? So we nursed the hangovers most of the day on Saturday before going to the college mixer on Saturday night, or perhaps to a movie. I'm speaking primarily of freshman or sophomore years. Many, many buddies shared the commiseration of all this.

Now, adult and maybe way beyond, I realize that there was a consequence to all this, and important at that. The habit of drinking alcohol with all its ramifications, some good, most bad, is something that I suspect many of us live with today.

The Friday nights in Kansas at one point turned out badly. One time, who knows how, we ended up at a different tavern in the Argentine district of Kansas City, Kansas. This at that time, and I can't speak for later, was a bad place to be, especially for some prep school or private college boys, most of whom had probably never looked for a fight in their short lives. We went into this bar and lo and behold there were some cute girls in the back booths. So after a few beers some dancing had started. Then all of a sudden the front doors opened wide and in came at least a half dozen pretty tough "dudes." We were told to get the hell out, but before a taxi could come, and this was in the age of no cell phones to call 911, some shoving and pushing took place and a few fists were thrown. One of our guys, somehow I remember he was from Chilicothe, Missouri, took a beer bottle to the head; it broke and a long scar became the souvenir. Somehow or other I escaped any harm but piled into the taxi, thinking as in "The Raven," "Never more!"

C. JUNIOR YEAR AT ROCKHURST

College now started to be more fun, notwithstanding the fun times already related. Study habits were established, and one's academic record was established. But one other reason for the added pleasure of being a junior at Rockhurst would be living in a different dorm up on the hill in old Sedgewick Hall. This is where the basketball jocks lived, and there was no Jesuit in residence, so we had a lot more freedom. I'll tell of dorm life in a bit, but a further factor was that I had a car on campus. I've mentioned the old "Pink tit," a 1953 Dodge with a "slushomatic" transmission; I think they called it Gyro Torque, an ugly vehicle but serving as great transportation for the next two years, the final ones at Rockhurst. There was one night, a frigid middle of the winter, when Abilene High School buddy Mike Kippenberger called and we all had a wonderful time drinking, partying and careening around frozen streets in the Dodge. It was at this time or perhaps later I believe when Mike was at Washburn University in Topeka, and together with fraternity brothers had come to Kansas City to party. Mike told of his cohorts at dental school who earned money part-time by being "night watchmen" at local funeral homes, and that the parties ended more than once with guys sleeping in and/or passed out in the caskets in the parlor.

Social life improved significantly but along the lines I have described: on the one hand there was the "normal" American life of dating girls I had met at St. Teresa's mixers. The dates were either to mixers or to an occasional movie, but it was certainly not a regular weekly occurrence due in some respects to a pretty limited budget. I think by now the cigarette job had gone by the way, but I still labored in the language lab as an assistant and made a little money, very little, with a new endeavor as a member of the "Blue Velvets," a lousy pre-rock band I joined in junior year.

1.   The Blue Velvets

The group was started by a fellow who lived in an extremely upscale area on the SW Kansas side of the city, maybe Shawnee Mission or other area. It was understood the family money came from condoms, manufacturing and selling them I mean. So I surmise there was no theological connection to life at Rockhurst, although I think he went there to school. Anyway, he was the lead guitarist, Phil Kezele on drums, Bill Bockelman on piano, I on rhythm guitar and perhaps another member or two. The band leader rounded up white tux coats and somebody's mother sewed collars of Blue Velvet and off we went. I think I wore dress slacks and loafers. What I did sport was a crew cut haircut (hair loss and balding were on their way, but as the college graduation photo showed, I had some time to go). We played the pop tunes of the times. I really can't remember many titles, but there were guitar solos, one the tricky "Guitar Boogie Shuffle" which I tried to master, emulating the head guitarist. I think I was allowed to slouch through a Duane Eddy twangy guitar song or two like "Honky Tonk." We played a local dance or two, but the big moment was in the spring when we traveled a considerable distance to Manhattan, Kansas, to play a fraternity party. You can imagine the talk from those times: a band from the big city, Kansas City! Big deal! So we got through that and made the astronomical sum of $25 each! After that I have no more memories. But it was a long drive home to the dorm.

2. Social Life with the Latinos and Latinas

The other side of the social coin was my ever increasing chumming around with the Latinos, all in an effort to learn Spanish. I really liked them and they certainly added spice to my life. There was the slick Guatemalan, Ernesto Townson (of the Townson-Granai Bank in Guatemala City), a Panamanian whom I knew in the dorm, but who wanted to speak only English and lay any chicks he could. On the Portuguese side there was Henrique Kerti for just one year before I graduated. It was first hearing Brazilian Portuguese from Henrique (his guttural box banging together sound of Carioca Portuguese on a long distance call home from the dorm lobby) and later beer drinking at Probasco's Dragon Inn up on Troost where Henrique would speak Portuguese and I would speak English and Spanish that cemented the friendship. Many encounters with Henrique and his family in Brazil would take place in later years.

But one of the truly good friends in life was from this period, Eduardo Matheu from Guatemala. I'll tell of my first trip to Guatemala and our adventures there later in this narrative.

It was through the Latinos that I met Latinas! Most of them were boarders at Notre Dame de Sion School for what turns out to be young ladies from very wealthy families in Latin America who wanted their daughters to learn French and English, do a bit of finishing and mainly be safe under the tutelage of the nuns who ran the place. All once again was very innocent; there was no "messing around" with these girls by any of us. I recall picnics and outings, lots of singing of Spanish songs (someone always had a guitar) and two events worth recounting.

I fell hard for one of the beauties from Mexico, Sylvia Reynal her name if I can recall all these years later. I think she tolerated my early efforts at Spanish, really not bad for a gringo, and we actually attended a dance or two. The culmination was the Notre Dame de Sion prom held in the ballroom of the Muelbach Hotel in downtown Kansas City, Missouri, perhaps the best hotel in town at the time. Sylvia was dressed in this formal gown, sparkling in appearance. She sparkled for another reason as well; she had returned from home near Chihuahua, Mexico, for the final spring term with a diamond engagement ring that you could not look at directly on a sunny day! So I was crushed, I suppose, but not really. I did not have that high of expectations. But for whatever reason, we still went to the ball. Surely I did not drive that old pink Dodge to the Muelbach. Maybe they rented a limo, no recollection of that.

A second event ties in with early lessons of real Hispanic culture, the ill-fated "serenata" or serenade for the young ladies of Notre Dame de Sion. The reader familiar with tradition from both Spain and Spanish America knows that the serenade is a wistful attempt by a young lover to impress his girl or fiancée of his great love by either singing, if he can, or hiring others to sing at the window of the object of his love. If she is awakened and likes what she hears, maybe she will toss him a rose, a symbol of her eternal love. I witnessed great serenades later on in Mexico as a young student in 1962. Who instigated the affair in 1962 in Kansas City I cannot say, but I was in the middle of it. I'm sure Ernesto Townson, Eduardo Matheu and others were the leaders, but I was the one with the guitar. After much fortification at a local tavern, we drove to the school, in a very nice area not far from the famous Plaza, parked, climbed over an iron gate or fence, proceeded to where we thought the girls' rooms were in their dorm and began our traditional Spanish serenade, including I'm sure "Las Mañanitas" the traditional serenade song, maybe "Cielito Lindo" and who knows what else. There were not many songs because we did not know many, but also because it was hard to sing with the barking of the dogs—Doberman watchdogs that quickly discovered us! In a matter of a few minutes the police arrived, red lights blinking, the dogs now really tuned up, and we were rounded up, told to be good boys and go on home and not come back. Once again, no charges were filed. Years later memories of that serenade would come back when I was in Brazil and Chico Buarque would sing his famous "Juca" and Jorge Amado would describe an epic serenade in "Dona Flor and her Two Husbands." One of the differences between Brazil and Spanish America was the Brazilians had another "serenade," different from the romantic serenading of the sweetheart, but on the beach at night with a fire, more like a Brazilian "Hootenanny".

Such was my social life during that fun junior year. The friendship with Eduardo would lead to one of the most memorable adventures in my young life the following summer when I would travel by Mexican bus to the border with Guatemala, across the beautiful highlands to Quetzaltenango and then on to Guatemala City where I would be introduced to an all too short vignette of upper class life in Latin America. I'll relate that in a moment.

3. Music and the Variety Show

It was junior year at Rockhurst that a really unforgettable series of events took place for me. All had to do with music and my aspirations for classic guitar, but also fun times with country music. I was self-taught with the classic guitar, but had learned some fairly sophisticated stuff which included a few selections of famous pieces from the masters in Spain. I practiced in the dorm room whenever I could, but can recall more the times after going out on Friday or Saturday night, returning to the dorm at let's say ten or eleven o'clock, taking the guitar (a Sears—Roebuck mail order job I bought for $50 dollars with earnings from the ice plant in the summers in Abilene) to a quiet room in the basement and playing perhaps for two or three hours at that quiet time. Such practice paid off, I guess, because I performed in a concert situation both junior and senior years at the annual Rockhurst Variety Show.

These memories are indelible: alone on stage, a few hundred people in the audience, no microphone, but with footstool and some courage, playing a few classics, including the obligatory "Malagueña," and receiving deafening applause for the effort. Nerves were a factor, but someone watched over me and I got through the pieces fine. I've played lots of classical guitar since at many student parties and most recently in a restaurant-bar in Durango Colorado, but never in that formal "concert" setting. Given my "iffens," since I could not be a pilot due to lousy vision and the brains for it, my second choice would have been to take the concert stage for classic guitar. Now, as I write this, I am older, wiser, and less idealistic. It may be best just to remember the "good ole days." This did not keep me from years later attending memorable concerts by the flamenco master Carlos Montoya, the "Royal Family of the Guitar" — the Romeros, Christopher Parkening and the daddy of them all, Andrés Segovia, performing at Gammage Auditorium at Arizona State University where I would teach for some 43 years.

Totally different but equally rewarding and certainly less nerve wracking was the country music parody I and a wonderful friend Bill Rost of Jefferson City, Missouri, would do for the variety show junior and senior years. It was "Curly and Slim's Noontime Jamboree," and I still have the worn, ragged one-page script. The perhaps 20 to 30 minute "show" was an incredible hit, surprisingly enough considering the audience was a non-country crowd of Jesuit college kids and faculty and their city relatives and friends.

Curly and Slim's Noontine Jamboree, Variety Show, Rockhurst College

Bill Rost, the "Slim" of the show (I with my balding pate was "Curly") was a natural ham, far more so than I who more often played the "straight" man to Bill's truly corny country jokes. But we hit the bull's eye on the parody, largely in part due to my early Abilene memories. The show was based on a real noon-time "Country Jamboree" at radio station KSAL in Salina, Kansas. The stars were local, of regional fame at best, but we incorporated almost all the parts of the show which ran 30 minutes each noontime. There was a theme song and some old classics like Hank Thompson's "I'm Moving on." We played the "Mom and Dad Waltz" for anniversaries; requests were always called or mailed in. "Keep those cards and letters comin' folks." Then came a birthday song, and there was always a spiritual at the end, generally "Just a Closer Walk with Thee." We were in tune, most of the time, me doing melody and Bill a pretty good harmonizer. But it was the corny jokes between us, the "palavering'" and the commercials that were the best.

The "business" side of the program was based on a real phenomenon growing up in Abilene. Gooch Best Feeds, a major source of prepared livestock feed was sold in 50 pound paper bags. Each bag had a red circle, worth points of course. You cut out the circles, kept them and when you had enough you could go to the annual Gooch Best Livestock Sale in the beautiful ranch country west of Salina, Kansas, for the auction. I never did have enough circles to matter much but did attend the auction for free hot dogs and soft drinks.

So our sponsor for the parody was Gooch's Best and we sold cattle feed, hog feed, chicken feed, duck feed and even "baby feed," egging on the audience to save those circle points. The show was full of letters (hilariously made up by Bill most of the time) from our radio audience. This was one of my happiest moments at Rockhurst, not just the successful shows themselves, but all those Saturday mornings in the dorm when we would practice, I surmise driving our buddies crazy. But they seemed to enjoy it too. I played an electric guitar with a small amplifier and Bill just sang. He was one of the few students at Rockhurst who were married and he and wife Rosie had a small apartment on the Paseo where we would hang out and drink a bit of beer. It was after graduation from Rockhurst, now a graduate student at Saint Louis University, when I would come through town to visit old cronies or on my way home to Abilene, and many a night Bill and Rosie would make up the divan for my bed. He went on to be a stalwart teacher and fund raiser at Bishop Miege High School in the Kansas City area, an English major who taught such stuff later on.

During all those practices in our dorm room on the third or fourth floor of old Sedgewick Hall, my roommate Denny Noonan was present. Denny was the one who helped me make it through Business Law senior year. A big tall redhead from St. Louis, Denny was infatuated with anything to do with John Wayne and we swore he even walked like the cowboy movie star. Denny was also enamored of the marines, went to officers' school immediately after Rockhurst, and ended up in Viet Nam. He survived the war but since then has never wanted to talk about it. A small aside, Denny had a new car at school, one of the few students with such good fortune, a white Chevy Nova. The Latinos got a few laughs out of that, because "No va" in Spanish means "it does not go." General Motors finally figured this out and did not try to sell it in Latin America. Denny became a good friend and also joined me as a guest for the 2000 dinner at Rockhurst I'll talk about later.

Because we were relatively short of funds, but with the smoking habit by now, there was a phase in the dorm life at Sedgewick Hall when one of the guys brought in a cigarette rolling machine, so we all got them, bought the papers and the tobacco in a pouch and rolled our own. It did not last long.

4. Folk Music, the Kingston Trio and the Limelighters

It was in these days that some kids had great stereo record players, the 33rpm was in vogue, and we were nuts for folk music, anything the Kingston Trio would be doing, but also a fine group called the Limelighters. A few fellows would perform their music in the aforementioned annual variety show. One of my few concert outings at Rockhurst was a trip by many of us to the auditorium at Kansas University in Lawrence for an unforgettable show by the Limelighters—Irish ballads by Glen Yarborough a famous tenor, many songs in other languages and the humor of the base player with his infamous rendition of "Have some Madeira my Dear." Many of these ditties I would learn for parties and performances later on.

One of the social moments junior year was the time I decided to stay in Kansas City for the Christmas holidays, probably cutting the umbilical from Abilene. Eduardo Matheu told of a good party on the Paseo with some TWA airline stewardesses. The problem was there was a blizzard, deep snow, too much to drive. We somehow found a sled, put my guitar on it, headed down the street to the Paseo, and went to the party. I guess I played the guitar, but certainly did not get the chance to go out with any stewardesses. Darn. I would not have known what to do if I had the chance.

5. Kansas City, the City and Diverse Events

During those years, it must have been junior or senior year; I would take the bus down Troost Avenue to downtown Kansas City, Missouri, passing by the famous 12th and Vine, and go to a fine music store with fine guitars. I would sit, play the best of the classic guitars, drool over them, but obviously did not have a dollar in my pocket to buy one. I still marvel they let me play them. Love for the guitar would culminate in December of 1966 when I bought my fine rosewood Di Giorgio Classic in the "Guitarra da Prata" in Rio de Janeiro, but that's another story for another book.

There was also sightseeing at the Plaza. Anyone in Kansas or Missouri knows of the beautiful Plaza shopping area in south Kansas City, Missouri. We would go there to window shop and maybe even find a place to drink a coffee or beer. An outstanding memory was the Saturday when Rockhurst buddies John Tobin, Jim Maloney and Paul Steichen went to the Plaza and begged for money. Somehow there were no arrests and they indeed did pick up a bit of pocket change. The Plaza deserved this—it was a snooty place at best.

The bus on Troost also took me at times to about 33rd and Troost, at the time a bit marginal part of town, but still relatively safe. I can recall going many times to the Isis Movie Theater to see some art films. A funny but not so funny aside: Senior year I took my date Ellen to the same theater to see Peter Sellers' "The Mouse that Roared." Innocent Ellen and perhaps as innocent Mark caught a double feature—the first film whose title I can't recall was a "date-night" doozy and whose contents were unknown to me prior to the evening. The only plot was a fellow put on a sort of 3-D glasses and saw all the women naked. Hmm. I recall his seeing a stenographer, a lady gardening, and that's it. We did stick around to see the "Mouse that Roared." Good for Ellen; she still went out with me later.

An important event, perhaps junior year, was the night several friends decided to go see a Kansas City Athletics baseball game down at the ball park on Brooklyn Avenue and 22nd Street. I've told that one of my main motives for attending Rockhurst was to live in Kansas City! Previous games at the park with my brother Jim and cronies and then one time with Abilene high school buddies had whetted my appetite for the sports and the city. That night John Tobin, Paul Steichen I think, maybe Jim Maloney and I took a bus to Brooklyn Avenue, the heart of the black section of Kansas City, took in a game and all was well. I guess to save money, someone, I don't know who, had the bright idea that we would walk back to Rockhurst. In those days, in those times you did not do this. There is no one to blame, but it was dangerous. And it was far, over thirty city blocks distant. We walked through the heart of the black section and somehow made it safely back to the dorm at white Rockhurst and lived to tell about it.

Beer drinking during junior and senior years now moved to the Missouri side up on Troost to the old Probasco Dragon Inn. It was not exactly a fancy place, but you could quaff a draft without too much nervousness of being carded. As mentioned in regard to friends from Latin America, it was here that I soon made a fine friendship with Henrique Kerti of Brazil. He would speak English and Portuguese, I would speak English and Spanish, so we understood each other most of the time. The friendship would blossom in Brazil with many visits to him and his family over many, many years. It was Henrique and his Portuguese that whetted my appetite for what would become a life-long career.

Shades of classic guitar! I still owe a favor to Arnold Dill, a classmate who was a whiz in mathematics and I think became one of those wizards who figure out life expectancy tables for insurance companies. Arnold one day casually mentioned to me, knowing my interest in classic guitar, "Hey, there is a guitar concert over at the UMKC [University of Missouri, Kansas City]; you might want to check it out."

The concert changed my life, at least part of it. The guitarist was a German, Sigfreid Behrund, and being on the circuit indicated that at least he was "middlin" to good. I thoroughly enjoyed the concert, but was in addition enthralled by his guitar case: he had decals from all over the world, ostensibly where he had performed. So I began to collect the decals in my limited travels to Mexico and such, and friends who went farther abroad collected them for me, particularly Dan Hayes of St. Louis days who traveled all over Europe. They adorn the case of my Di Giorgio Classic from the "Guitarra da Prata" in Rio de Janeiro yet today. But the concert was a first and whetted my appetite for more.

6. Classes and Academics Junior Year

I have already commented on teachers, good and bad, lay and Jesuit. Suffice to say at this point I was doing very well in most courses, but my heart was in the Spanish classes of Vernon Long, mentor and friend. I probably was doing an introduction to Spanish Literature at the time. Friendships with the Latinos and practice speaking Spanish were foremost. I think I was Honor Roll and all the rest. But then a life-changing event took place. Professor Long had a heart to heart talk with me and gave me some invaluable advice. He said that in the future, I as an Anglo learning Spanish as a second language would only be able to compete in the future, either in graduate school in Spanish or in business in Latin America, if I were to have experience in a Spanish speaking country. There I could better my oral facility. So we checked it out and came to the conclusion that a summer in Mexico City, being the closest and most reasonable, and summer school at the National University of Mexico [Universidad Nacional de México] might do the trick. It was my first international experience, a true odyssey to the Spanish speaking world and it did indeed change my life. Because such an experience is a part of life and formation for so many young college students, and was much rarer at that time, that adventure should be part of this narrative.

PART II.
MEXICO CITY, THE NATIONAL UNIVERSITY OF MEXICO AND INTRODUCTION TO GUATEMALA

A. MEXICO AND THE NATIONAL UNIVERSITY

1. Why and How

The story is long and perhaps not too interesting to accustomed world travelers, but there are many young Americans who did such things that changed their lives. Here is the story in great or lesser detail. It is only slightly edited from the original hand written travel diary of 1962. This journal of the trip seems to me to be extremely naïve and certainly a product of a twenty year old. But for any youngster about to face that strange, new world of study, travel and growing up a bit, there are moments worth sharing. Looking back on the trip of some fifty years ago, I marvel a bit at what I did and that I survived with no accidents, robberies, sickness or worse. My diary reveals many fundamental things about the country and people of Mexico and Guatemala and a bit about growing up.

So this is the trip that started it all. By "all" I mean graduate studies and a job for the next forty-three years. I was between junior and senior years at Rockhurst College in Kansas City, Missouri, fresh off the farm in Abilene. The largest city I had spent any time in was Kansas City, at that time perhaps one million total population in the greater metropolitan area. Most of my time even in that middle sized city was spent on 55 acres of campus—the dorm, the cafeteria, the classrooms and the language lab at Rockhurst. My major in college was Business Management, all because I was scared to death of the science and math requirements for the B.A. degree, but I had a minor in Spanish. I did well in the latter by virtue of good structural preparation in high school in Abilene with Miss Edna Edberg, the proverbial schoolmarm, taking Latin and Spanish from her. I grew in knowledge and skills in Spanish at college with Professor Vernon Long from New Orleans and LSU, having described him and the classes previously in this book. Outside of class I learned a lot by associating with the Latinos on campus, largely from Mexico, but with a smattering from Peru, Ecuador, Guatemala and Costa Rica.

Mexico was the closest and most reasonable choice for a language immersion experience. With my Dad's help I took out a loan for $500 at 3 per cent interest at the Abilene National Bank to pay for the summer. Incidentally, I was one of the ones who paid off my federally guaranteed loan years later after graduate school with the interest by then almost matching the principal. I bought a one-way bus ticket from Kansas City, Missouri, to Mexico City, D.F. (Federal District). It cost in the neighborhood of $50 in those days, coincidentally the number of hours of the trip, and the few hundred dollars left from the loan were intended for tuition at the U.N.A.M., books and living expense in Mexico City. Green, with the hayseed coming out of my ears, and most of all, naïve, I set off. As a parent today I can only surmise my small town, farm parents' anxiety over the endeavor. People of great faith and evidently some trust in their son!

2. The Bus Trip

"The bus route in the U.S. from Kansas City to the Mexican border was all new to me: Joplin, Tulsa, Dallas, Waco, Austin, San Antonio and finally Laredo, Texas, on the border with Mexico. I recall having to sit next to a bum along the route to Tulsa and next to a bragging, Negro cowboy around San Antonio (shades of "Blazing Saddles," one of my all-time Mel Brooks' favorites). Among the many stops, one recollection was of the separate facilities for blacks and whites in Waco, including the drinking fountain. Another strong impression was the incredible number of Spanish-speaking people in and around San Antonio; I felt like I was already in a foreign country. A vague memory still is how pretty San Antonio was with the course of the river through town.

"The memory is in charge (with the help of my travel notes). Still in the U.S., I was amazed by the terrain of south Texas, the broad stretches with little more than brown grass and cactus. Kansas with its green fields and generally productive appearance was my only point of comparison. Another flashback was of the all black towns we passed through in Oklahoma and Texas, my first experience with that remaining vestige of the past. There is in north central Kansas by the way a tiny town called Nicodemus which was an all-Negro community and is now a national historic site.

An aside: These notes seem pretty sketchy to me now; they are 49 years old as I retype them on the computer. That is another reason to write now; I am sure the memories will fade even more as time goes by.

"We changed bus lines at Laredo, Texas, waiting in line and trying to find my baggage. I think I took one large suitcase and a trunk if you can imagine that! The moment was a revelation to me since it was all in Spanish, my first shocking immersion into the language. There was some difficulty in finding the luggage, so I was last getting on the bus of "Transportes del Norte" which was in fact an intermediate bus taking us across the border to the Nuevo Laredo, Mexico, checkpoint. The border was of course the river, the Río Grande or Río Bravo, as you like.

"Arriving "on the other side," I was, I surmise, in total culture shock the whole time; there seemed to be mass confusion as we had to open all the luggage and then check visas or tourist cards. Perhaps, in retrospect, my large suitcase and trunk may have seemed a bit unusual to the border officials considering I just had a tourist visa for two or three months. Things might have moved a bit faster had I known or thought of providing a "tip" to the Mexican customs people ["Aduana"] or to the bus driver himself! They transferred me to another bus, but I was called off to go and open my trunk once again for the inspectors. The end result was I was exhausted and very upset for the hassle, and sweaty hot from it all. I was rewarded with the back seat in the bus from the border all the way to Mexico City; there was no place to put my carry-on luggage and the bus was hot as an oven. An oracle for future bus trips in Latin America?

"About fifty miles outside of Laredo there was another checkpoint, but this time there was no request to open luggage. The Mexican bus ride continued (see the great Spanish filmmaker Luis Buñuel's classic "Mexican Bus Ride" sometime). We passed through several little towns, now traveling at night. The most I wanted to try at that point was a Coke! There was, by the way, a very specific scent proper to those towns, not offensive but different, unlike anything up North. I knew I was not on the farm in Kansas. We passed through Monterrey, a huge industrial city with a major university, the "Tecnológico de Monterrey," and San Luis de Potosi where there were mariachis on the streets at that very early hour and where I had my first Mexican "café con leche" which I was totally unaccustomed to and thought bad tasting. Later the bus careened through San Juan del Río, Querétaro and finally arrived at the outskirts of Mexico City!

3. Arrival in Mexico City, a Bit of Chaos, and Some Good Fortune

"At first sight I did not care at all for México City; it seemed dry, dirty and everything appeared to be slums, this <u>circa</u> 1962. We passed "Ciudad Satélite" and one of the large bull rings on the way to the city center or downtown. It turns out that indeed they had had an unusual dry spell in the Valley of Mexico which was broken shortly after we arrived with daily rain thereafter.

"A fellow bus passenger from Honduras helped me and Leonor a girl from Detroit who was on my bus and who was going to attend the UNAM to find a taxi. There was mass confusion at the huge downtown bus depot in Mexico City. I'm fairly sure we got the run-around by the taxi driver, but efficiently noted the taxi ride cost 14 pesos, $1.16 U.S. Leonor and I were told later the fare should have been only three or four pesos. The pesos would add up quickly, and even $500 US would not have sufficed for my summer experience had I not run into some good luck later. The reason for the actual cheap taxi fare and not our inflated price was that our hotel was indeed within a block or two of the bus depot, and the "chofer" indeed had driven us in circles. All this was more than mildly unsettling to yours truly, a "gringo" in culture shock.

"I stayed at the Versalles Hotel in downtown, the place suggested by friends in Kansas City. It was clean, nice, middle range and even offered a courtesy cocktail upon arrival, a margarita or something, a first-time experience for the Kansas farm boy.

4.   First and Only Contact: the Maravillos

"From the hotel I called my only contact in Mexico City, no easy matter. The first telephone conversation in a second language is a momentous occasion for all language students. The call was to Carlos Maravillos Baez, my only connection in Mexico by virtue of mutual friends at Rockhurst, Cliff and his wife from Guatemala. It turned out there was no trouble at all with this first phone conversation, that is, the Spanish and communicating, a definite plus after all the years in the classroom. Carlos lived very close to the hotel, within walking distance. I did not realize it then, but his was an incredible location in 1962; we were near the "Zona Rosa" the upper end shopping area of downtown Mexico City. Carlos' home was on Calle Londres and down the street would be the residence of the U.S. ambassador where President John F. Kennedy and his famous wife Jackie would stay during a momentous visit later that summer.

Mark and Carlos Maravillos, Paseo de la Reforma, Mexico City

"It was a short jaunt to the famous Paseo de la Reforma, a beautiful sight with all its plazas or "glorietas," one with the statue of Cuautémoc, the final Aztec leader during the battle with the future conqueror of Mexico, the Spaniard Hernán Cortés in 1519-1521. Yet another "glorieta" had the "Ángel de la Independencia" with its golden wings. Farther down on the Paseo was Chapúltepec Park and the forest, "Bosque de Chapúltepec." It was an incredible piece of good fortune to be so centrally located to the famous and pleasant sites in Mexico. After that walk and introduction, I headed back to my hotel, the middle class Versalles.

The National Cathedral, Mexico City

"The next day was Sunday and I went to mass with Carlos' family in the National Cathedral of Mexico in the Zócalo, the main plaza in old Mexico City. The cathedral was huge, beautiful, the largest in the Americas. The twenty year old from Kansas had never seen anything like it. The mass was the same as at home, pre-Vatican II: the priest faced the altar, his back to the people, and the mass was in Latin. The men, young and old, stood in the back as opposed to sitting or kneeling on the hard wooden kneelers like the women and children. Many of them seemed to drift outside to smoke during the sermon; considering the speaker system and my bookish Spanish, I should have joined them. There were very few communions as opposed to current practice in the U.S. at the time.

"We returned to Carlos' house for dinner at about two p.m. and watched the bullfights on TV that afternoon. That afternoon I took the guitar over to Carlos' house, played and sang; all was very enjoyable. (Query: did I haul that damned guitar all the way from Abilene on the trip? I think so.)

5. Introduction to the National University of Mexico [La Universidad Nacional Autónoma de México, la U.N.A.M.]

"June 18. Monday. Carlos took me and Leonor Holland and Janet Maker, all lodgers at my hotel, to the National University. There was no time yet for tourism. We were required to take a language placement test; I took the "superior" or advanced and was gently told I would be better off in the Intermediate II. I paid my $100 tuition (about 1249 pesos) and then set off to find a place to stay in the city. The summer school kept lists for all foreigners. There were lots of señoras at the school itself trying to get us to visit their house and stay with them. I looked at three places, one of which I liked. Prices ranged from 700-950 pesos per month. Speaking of this situation to the Maravillos, Carlos invited me to stay with them. From today's perspective, knowing a bit more now of Latino customs, I am still not sure if this was the "expected" offer of hospitality or the "serious" offer. At any rate, I jumped at the chance and took it. It turned out that the house is owned by Carlos' mother-in-law [suegra]. Everyone seemed to be in agreement, so I moved in, a very pleasant arrangement as far as I could see. They gave me a private room, and I do not know yet how that was arranged, since the place was not overly large — naiveté again. The Indian maid washed all my clothes! I in effect would live like a king. Carlos, his wife Elena who is expecting in September, their very young son, and a very likable cousin and a brother-in-law also lived there. "The food has been fine with three meals per day. Breakfast cooked to my liking by the Indian maid: bacon, eggs, juice, toast and coffee. The main meal was at two o'clock p.m.: generally there was meat, rice or potatoes, bread, vegetables, fruits of all kinds (I recall the papaya). Then at around 8:30 at night came the "cena" which is light: lunch ham, tortillas, hot sauce, frijoles, rice, "panitos" and jelly, and coffee. After dinner we would generally watch TV."

6. Life in the Federal District (D.F.)

"Wednesday, June 20. I slept late, went to the post office with a letter home, ate dinner, and not much else. There was time later on to look around on the Paseo and go to a movie for 8 pesos (64 cents US): SPARTACUS with Kirk Douglas, at the most expensive movie house [cine] in Mexico City located on the Paseo de la Reforma before Chapúltepec. Then came a bit of a dicey scene: I met this Mexican on the Paseo, walked around town with him, and met his brother. I was later scolded by the Maravillos to be careful of the thieves [rateros]. You can take the boy out of the country . . .

"Thursday. I went on a bit of a wild goose chase to look up Alberto Silva, another of my few contacts in Mexico City, a close friend of my Rockhurst friend from Guatemala Eduardo Matheu. As you might expect his was a beautiful home; he was very cordial and invited me to a party the coming Sunday. "I think he will be a very good friend, very hospitable." I got lost coming back from Alberto's house, met two American girls from Florida in the same fix, both going to the summer school at the UNAM, so will probably see them on Monday when classes begin. I ended up taking a taxi home, tired from all the walking in circles.

Lord, the innocence, the naiveté, was someone watching over my shoulder? Even then Mexico City probably was a metropolis of 15 million folks, and not all of them were good, upstanding citizens keeping an eye out for naïve gringos.

"Friday, June 20. I slept until 9 a.m., and Carlos and I went to meet my "friend" I met the other day on the Paseo. Carlos wanted to check him out. We went to the "centro" to a music store, a guitar shop where I played my first Mexican guitar. Soon a crowd was gathering around listening. An adult and a little boy even asked my advice on what type of guitar to buy. The guitars were inexpensive, from US 7 to 10$, but a good one for solo work is about the same as in the U.S. That turned out to be the last encounter with the acquaintance, duly forewarned was I by Carlos. What do I know? It turns out he was poor, perhaps sincere in making an American friend, but the Maravillos were not at all trusting of the different class situation.

"Later . . . I took my first "pesero" back from the Zócalo this morning. (Years later I would read "Where the Air is Clear" ["La Región Más Transparente"] by Carlos Fuentes with the narrative voice that of the driver ["chofer"] of the "pesero.") These are taxis which charge one peso, 8 cents US, for fares up and down the Paseo and/or Insurgentes, the two main avenues in the city. The Zócalo is at one end of the Paseo; Chapúltepec Park is at the other. Later I would read that during the French occupation of Mexico in the 1860s with Archduke Maximiliano and his wife Carlota in charge, supposedly Carlota made Maximiliano construct the Paseo so she could be sure he would come straight home from work from the Zócalo! Carlos' home is just two blocks off the Paseo. The buses that summer cost 40 centavos or 3 cents U.S.! More on the "peseros:" you stand at the curb, hold up one finger and wait for one to stop. They were painted red and were real wrecks, 1949 Chevys or Fords, often with one door wired shut, the front windshield filled with decorations, the dashboard with a statue of Our Lady of Guadalupe, or perhaps a nude woman. It was always a scramble to get one. But there was no "Plastic Jesus on the Dashboard of My Car."

7.   "Observations to This Point"

(Get this! My Lord! The text is in quotations direct from the diary of a twenty year old.)

"People are generally nice; there are definitely two social classes with a growing, budding middle class. Many slums exist in the city. You can see workers with old, patched clothing and shoes with holes in them. You see Indians who come into the city to sell their handicrafts ["artesanías"] to folks. People are generally dark skinned, but frequently light skinned, mostly the upper classes I surmise, originally "criollos" or "españoles.""

"Most folks go to work at 8, 9, or 10 a.m., come home for the main meal at 2 p.m. and return to work at 4 p.m. Then they are off work at 6 or 7 p.m. Most take buses to work, or taxis. They may have a car but do not drive it because of the traffic and lack of parking facilities. Most cars are foreign, U.S. or European, and luxury Mercedes are seen very often. Local folklore has it that the concessions for Mercedes in Mexico are connected to Mexico's current President Adolfo López Mateos! The traffic scene described is of course all pre-metro or subway.

"Home: It may be a room, an apartment or an entire house. All the homes are kept tightly locked with "rejas," iron latticework covering all the windows and front yards that is, if they have them, and with tall walls ["murallas"] in front. From the street it is difficult to tell how nice the house is because the outsides all appear to be quite old. Once inside the front gate or door, the difference is easily seen. Some places are wrecks, dirty, old, and broken down. Others are nice and I have seen one or two richly furnished with all the best furniture and appliances.

"Entertainment. "Futbol" is the most popular sport, then "béisbol." American football is not popular at all, even though there is one well-known American-style football team from the UNAM and there is a small league. The bull fight is still popular in Mexico, but is slowly losing in popularity to soccer. The latest news here is of the World Cup of Soccer. Brazil won; Mexico did well; you see the sports clips in the cinema. The championship has become a symbol of national prestige.

"Movies are extremely popular and can be afforded by all classes. Most cinemas charge 4 pesos, 32 cents US, but in the "barrios" they are even cheaper. The old movie houses are built in splendid fashion along the line of the old Loew's or Orpheum chains in the U.S. (the Fox in St. Louis is along this line). It is strange to be in such plush surroundings when one thinks of the class structure that exists in Mexico. The cinemas are always super crowded, I surmise due to the very inexpensive admission price. There are many movie theaters along the Paseo and Insurgentes, but also "teatros" or theaters for plays and variety shows. Most impressive is the Palace of Fine Arts ["Palacio de Bellas Artes"], home of the national symphony and the "Ballet Folclórico de México." It is known for the glass curtain, ["cortina de vidrio"] and later, I learned, for one of Diego Rivera's famous murals, the one destroyed in Rockefeller Center due to the image of Lenin which Rivera refused to remove. Photos were taken, and he recreated it in Bellas Artes.

"It was also a custom in 1962 to go on a picnic outside the city. Folks with cars did this, and those without arranged pesero taxis or buses to the sites. In the city Chapúltepec Park was a great gathering place for picnics on the weekends.

"Buying habits. (Is this a "hoot" or not?) "This is very superficial knowledge on my part, but impressions of a twenty-year old foreigner. This is one of the most interesting of the topics. I write as I think it appeared to me. All kinds of stores exist, modern department stores of all kinds, chain stores, and especially the "hole in the wall" "tienda" which sells food, sweets, tobacco, drinks and ice cream. I used the latter to buy cigarettes and also for a daily "Dos Equis" after getting home from the university at around noon, shortly before the "almuerzo" at two o'clock. The bottle of beer was two pesos! They have what seems like thousands of street vendors who sell everything from ice cream to tacos to knife-sharpening devices. A separate chapter in itself is the "boleros" or shoe shine boys/men. I could even afford this! There is one large department store near us, the "Steel Palace" ["Palacio de Hierro."] It is modern with many imported products. Prices here seem to be comparable or higher than in the U.S. Every other small shop seems to be a jewelry shop or a tourist souvenir shop.

8.   Life in D.F., Continued

"Saturday, June 23. I went with Carlos' cousin Ricardo to Insurgentes to Las Américas Cine where we saw "Los Valientes Andan Solos," a classic Kirk Douglas film of a modern cowboy escaping the law and modern law enforcement along the U.S.-Mexican border, a story of a man and his horse versus the police and helicopters. A curious note: in the final scene there is a truck bearing down on the cowboy, just at the point of making it safely across the border into Mexico. The truck driver is none other than Carroll O'Connor of Archie Bunker fame. Only later did I learn that the story or the screen play was done by Edward Abbey of "Desert Solitaire" fame.

"That night we went to Ricardo's brother-in-law's house and played poker, in Spanish I dare say, until 3 a.m. Games were "poker a la mesa," "no se ven," and "comodín." Eight people played and the gringo lost 9 pesos.

The Villa de Guadalupe, Mexico City

"Sunday, June 24th. Classes begin tomorrow. We got up late, no surprise, and went to mass at the Villa de Guadalupe, the national shrine to the Virgin who appeared to the Indian Juan Diego in about 1521. As the story goes, she instructed Juan Diego to have a shrine built upon the spot. He went to the church officials, reporting the vision, but they did not believe his story. She reappeared to him offering to mark the spot with roses. No roses grew there normally, but at that moment some budded forth. He gathered them, put them in a shawl ["rebozo"] and when he opened the "rebozo" later before the Bishops, her image was on it. This is the image and portrait of the "Virgen de Guadalupe" that is enshrined today and is reproduced on images throughout the Catholic world. At the time there was a large courtyard ["atrio"] surrounding the original church and a small shrine on the hill behind the courtyard. Outside the iron lattice work ["rejas"] surrounding the large atrium there are crowds of vendors selling all manner of things—pictures of the Virgin, candy of all sorts, fruit, vegetables and "terrible stinking meat." Mariachis and other solo musicians with guitars play for a price. And there are also stage props where you can have your picture taken with the cardboard Virgin!

"The church I saw in 1962 was the original in the style of old 17th century Mexican baroque, rough and dirty on the outside, but ornate and beautiful on the inside. Since Mexico City is built on a lake bed ["El Lago de Texcoco"] of the Aztecs, the church is slowly sinking into the ground, and at a very severe angle." An aside: only some 30 years later would my wife Keah and I visit the shrine, now converted into an ultra-modern basilica where one stood in long lines to pass by the original "rebozo" of the Virgin in a glass case high above. The shrine/basilica is huge with thousands of worshipers. And a plethora of vendors, musicians, and even con-artists lurk outside awaiting humble Mexicans from the interior as well as big-eyed tourists.

In the back of today's shrine, on a hill above the current modern church, is a beautiful shrine and from the top of the hill in 1962 one could see on the day we visited a beautiful view of Mexico City and surrounding mountains, contrasting to the intense smog Keah and I saw in 2000.

"I seemed to be the only gringo there that day amongst thousands of Mexicans, mostly poor and many of Indian descent. In the courtyard below the church traditional Indian dances were presented with very colorful costumes, all for donations. My impression: "It was beautiful but totally commercialized and it seemed a sacrilege for such a holy place."

I think, now in 2011, there is some interesting perspective in all this. I saw the same commercialization on the streets leading to Fatima in Portugal, Lourdes in France and even St. Peter's in Rome, years later. Not to mention the bazaars of Turkey outside the Sulimaniye Blue Mosque in Istanbul.

"We later returned home to once again watch the bullfights on TV.

"Monday, June 25th. There are no classes yet today, so another American guy and I went with two girls we met at school to Coyoacán a part of town near the university. It was very beautiful with a colonial church; we had lunch in a colonial style restaurant as well, "El Convento." An aside: a few years later I would learn that Coyoacán was famous for the residence "The Blue House," [la Casa Azul] of Frida Kahlo and Diego Rivera, but I was ignorant of all this in 1962.

"Tuesday, June 26. Classes started. All were okay except one—Latin American Literature—too demanding for my language preparation level in1962. That night Carlos, Ricardo and I went to a "Variedades" show in the downtown. This is the Mexican version of our old vaudeville plus a bit of "Broadway.""

"Thursday. I changed classes, dropping the difficult Latin American Literature and a conversation course, not worthwhile in my estimation, but enrolling in two other "cracker—jack" courses I'll talk more of later. The gringo actually had a real date that night with Linda Rogers of Gainsville, Florida, and we naively lolled in and around the Zócalo."

"Friday. No classes. Indeed this was all due to a huge event! President John F. Kennedy and wife Jacqueline are in town. I went to the Paseo de la Reforma and along with an estimated one and one-half million others saw the Kennedys ride in a limousine convertible down the Paseo from the airport. The president of Mexico Adolfo López Mateos rode with them. Kennedy seemed older, a bit grayer than the images from the campaign debates on television in the U.S. I later walked to the U.S. Embassy, amazingly only some three or four blocks up the street from my hosts' house on Calle Londres. All the women in the crowd were shouting, "Queremos a Jackie; queremos a Jackie!" That night I was at the movies in Chapúltepec Cine and there was an extensive newsreel on the Kennedys' visit. Whenever Jackie appeared on screen there was vast cheering and whistling." An aside: During this time in Mexico and the Kennedy visit there was an atmosphere of hope, all positive toward the U.S. These were the days of the Alliance for Progress ["Alianza para el Progreso"] the good neighbor program launched by Kennedy shortly after his inauguration in 1961, a true partnership for the economic development of Latin America. There has been nothing like it since, and absolutely nothing comparable to Kennedy's popularity and the all-time good relations the U.S. had with Mexico. One recalls he would be assassinated just one year later. The Alliance along with the Peace Corps marked the heady moments in international relations, and we young students of Spanish and Latin America cherished them both. A bit of an aside: Jacqueline spoke some Spanish, her main language being Eastern Boarding School French; she spoke in a very soft, semi-sexy voice, definitely with a foreign accent, but was loved by all. Years later I would try to imitate this voice in a parody of the lady while telling stories in Spanish classes at ASU.

"Saturday. I saw the Kennedy's again at the portico of the Embassy; there was a huge crowd and many speeches. In retrospect, the small town farm boy had now met Dwight D. Eisenhower in 1952 when Ike opened his presidential campaign in Abilene (I told of this in "The Farm"), now Kennedy in 1962 and just one year later would witness a memorable encounter with former president Harry Truman to be told later in this book.

"Local customs and color. Strolling singers or minstrels will get aboard a bus on Insurgentes, ride a few blocks, sing a song or two, pass the hat and get off. They provided very good entertainment most of the time." An aside: The only thing like this I ever witnessed in the U.S. was the bus to

ASU still in teaching days when a huge black fellow would imitate Aretha Franklin and the whole stable of rhythm and blues singers. He should have asked for money.

"Sunday July 1. We went to mass in a neighboring church on the Reforma. Then the family, Carlos, Elena, la señora, their son Julio and I and Dave Tickmeyer, colleague at the UNAM, went to Toluca in the family car. A Sunday outing. The scenery was beautiful with mountains, pine forests and valleys. Toluca (71,000) is famous for the Sunday market (little did I realize I would "live" in the markets in Brazil years later). I wrote, "They sell everything including all kinds of chile peppers and, 'ugh, bad food.'" We looked all around the market and, if one can believe it, bought a serape! It cost 42 pesos, US $3.92, fitting my budget nicely. I bargained with the vendor who settled for two thirds of the original asking price of 60 pesos. Local wisdom is to start the bargaining at half the first asking price and meet somewhere in between. We ate outside of town and returned via a park in the mountains outside of Mexico City." I can only surmise what is left today of the scenery of that beautiful drive in 1962. The park was beautiful with dense forest, the prettiest landscape I had seen thus far in Mexico. We passed by the ruins of an old convent making me think of the famous Spanish Romantic Play "The Force of Destiny ["La Fuerza del Sino"] with its convents and the final scene when the tragic hero Don Alvaro finds himself on a precipice, decides to end it all, and jumps off the cliff while speaking a romantic line of the times. He shouts "Infierno!! Trágame!" ["Hell, devour me."] So this is what a ride in the country past an old convent does for a Spanish Major.

"The family likes to do these Sunday outings; they are speaking possibly of Puebla next week. Alas, it did not happen." Of note is that the family car was a sparkling new Ford; the señora, a widow, has money from the old religious object factory in Michoacán, its specialties being silver coin reproductions of the Aztec Sun Calendar and images of the Virgin of Guadalupe. It was "campy" tourist stuff to be sure, but a big business success.

"A political and diplomatic note of the times. During a regular day of classes I attended a program at the U.S. Embassy, a lecture on the "Chamizal" problem, a topic of great emotional importance to Mexico. The "Chamizal" is a strip of land at El Paso where the Río Grande had changed course, moving to the south, thus taking land away from Mexico. The solution of the treaty was to give the land back to Mexico resulting in a "diplomatic and symbolic victory" for Mexico and a betterment of international relations. Keeping in mind that the U.S. basically annexed one half of Mexico after the U.S. Mexico war of the 1840s, the "Chamizal" was indeed insult added to injury and a bitter cup of tea for Mexico until its resolution in 1962.

"The days pass. There were classes and a date that afternoon with Barbara Murphy, her father in management for Maxwell House. We ate, walked through Chapúltepec, and went to a movie."

"At some point I saw "Psycho" with Anthony Perkins."

Mark in the Spanish Picaresque Novel Class, the National University of Mexico

"Thursday. By now I have excellent classes with the Spanish Picaresque Novel ["Novela Picaresca"] and the prose of Cervantes. I shall tell more on them in a bit. That night the family went by car to Garibaldi Plaza to hear mariachi music. It is "drive-in" style: you park alongside the plaza, contract a mariachi group to play a song, pay up and listen. An altogether new experience, the episode evoked a funny thought or two when I could not help but recall the drive-in movies in Abilene in the 1950s."

"Friday. I'm with fellow student Ron from Big Springs, Texas, and we go to a wedding reception. He dressed in leather cowboy jeans and matched the clothing with a Texas accent in Spanish. He said that back home they drive 100 miles out of his dry county to buy beer in another. Such is the thirst in dry Texas. In Kansas at least we could quaff weak 3.2 Coors.

"Sunday. There is another jaunt with the family, in this instance to Cuernavaca, my first time of course. After lunch we climbed a small hill which had a terrific view of the city. Weather was as advertised—perfect! (Cuernavaca is known as the land of "eternal springtime" in the tourist brochures.) We drove through town, saw the small square and market and to its side the Palace of Cortez [Palacio de Cortés] decorated with Diego Rivera murals." At the time I was totally unaware of their importance. Once again only in more mature student days and even teaching days would I come to know of and appreciate these important aspects of Mexican culture.

Mark in Front of the National Palace, Mexico City

Diego Rivera's Mural, "History of Mexico," the National Palace, Mexico City

Rivera employed a style criticized as "comic book murals," but described more correctly by most critics as a realism depicting the Marxist dialectic. He would in effect create in these murals and more importantly those in the National Palace in Mexico City his "History of Mexico." He was one among three or four major artists, like Siqueiros or Orozco, in the Mexican Muralist Movement, public art sponsored by the Mexican government to teach and praise of the ideals of the Revolution of 1910. Once one becomes aware of such things one can then appreciate, for example, the beautiful mosaics of the library at the U.N.A.M. which also depict past and present history of Mexico.

"The next week. The days pass in what has become routine. I attended classes, studied, and played "Monopolía" with Carlos' and Elena's young son Julio; I guess the game is international. I went to the Museum of History [Museo Histórico de Chapúltepec,] "a big deal for the Mexicans." The historic site remembers the war with the United States, the invasion of our marines at Vera Cruz, and then the defense of Mexico City by the heroic young martyrs — high school teens of the military academy of Chapúltepec. Needless to say the version presented was quite a bit different than anything I had heard about the US-Mexican War in the U.S.

"Saturday. We went again to Chapúltepec, but his time to the "zoológico," a really fine zoo in a pretty setting. That night I played poker again and saw "el box." Boxing is extremely popular in Mexico City, and the Mexicans are very nationalistic about it; most fighters seemed to be in the "gallo" or light weight division. I do not know if that major popular cultural phenomenon of modern day Mexico, the wrestling heroes, was going on then, but boxing always was huge in the sports pages and on television.

Pyramid of the Sun, Teotihuacán, Mexico

Sunday. The day marked my introduction to Teotihuacán, the site and name of one of Mexico's most impressive Pre-Colombian cultures. I would study this culture in great detail years later, visit the site again on two occasions and teach about it in my Latin American Civilization classes at ASU. It preceded the later Toltec and Aztec civilizations and was contemporary to the early Mayan period and a bit before the Zapotec culture near Oaxaca at Monte Albán. In one sense it was a Proto-Culture ["proto-cultura"] compared to others in Mexico. The outing once again combined tourism with a family "picnic." As I recall all this fifty years later and check my notes, it is amazing all I saw and did in those few short introductory weeks in a country and with a people I would study intensely years later. Who would have thought? ["Quién hubiera dicho?"] We of course saw the two main pyramids, "La Pirámide del Sol" and "La Pirámide de la Luna." One needs today to recall scenes from "Frida" with Frida Kahlo and Leon Trotsky atop the Pyramid of the Moon. We climbed to the top of both pyramids, both very steep, very impressive, especially "El Sol." Again, at the time I knew very little about Teotihuacán, but recall standing on the apex of the big pyramid. There were storm clouds brewing all across the valley and it was very windy and a bit frightening being exposed to the elements at that height. Only years later would I learn that the principal god of the site was in fact a goddess, of water! The pyramid of the Moon at that time was not excavated! It was a very historic time to be there.

"The family had a "comida típica" style picnic, the food washed down with a lot of tequila with "sal y limón." Memories therefore are a bit fuzzy. We ate tacos, carnitas, and chicharrones. We hunted for rocks and found an arrow head and Aztec pottery (Carlos says they "plant" these "arqueological finds" for the tourists.) Who knows? I took pictures with a tiny camera on loan from the family. The Pyramid of the Sun is 75 meters high. We also walked along the main avenue of the site [La ciudadela] and saw the temple dedicated to agriculture and the "Templo de Quetzalcoátl," the winged-feathered serpent. It rained as we returned to the city." All this seems odd, quaint, and naïve to me now after seriously studying it all in later years. I recall immense bus and tourist traffic to the site even then. One can only imagine today in 2011.

"Monday. A Mexican happening: this was a small but great Mexican cultural moment and authentic to boot! I awoke at 6:00 a.m. to the sound of mariachis; they were serenading the girl next door on her birthday. There were about eight of them dressed in Mexican rodeo outfits ["charro" outfits]; they played outside first and then entered the house. The little lady of course lived on the second floor and if tradition has it correctly, should have thrown a rose or two down on her singers (perhaps accompanied by a suitor, but in this case I think all was organized by the family for the birthday). That same day I became interested in watching the day laborers who toiled on a street project in front of the house. They paused now and again to drink a pale fluid from what looked like Mason Jars. Carlos informed it was not water but "pulque" used to fortify them and get them through the day. (Perhaps akin to the coca leaves the farm workers and laborers in mines high in the Andes still use today for a similar purpose.)

The next day I complained: "I had to take a cab to school today. Got tagged for $1.50 US." Our house was far, far from the university!

"Rest of the week: routine. I had a date with Carol Irwin of El Paso, Texas; we doubled with Ron and Peggy and went to "El Rincón de Goya" in the Zona Rosa near El Paseo. I can't believe the places we went on my budget! The restaurant, as one surmises by the name, was Spanish style with flamenco dancers, flamenco guitar, and various strolling minstrels. The waiters "shined" in their "suits of lights" ["traje de luces"] as in bull fights, and wore an interesting accouterment of hair nets. The gringos all enjoyed a good steak dinner at a reasonable price. Then we marched off to the Hilton on the Paseo with mariachi bands, then to the Hotel del Paseo with its terrace and view of the city from high above. The latter was very impressive, and it cost me 20 pesos! Imagine! ["Imagínate!"]

"Saturday. Back to Chapúltepec Park where we rowed canoes, 5 pesos per hour!

Mark in Language Class, National University of Mexico, 1962

"Sunday. I studied and read novels for class." With all the tourism, eating and drinking described, it is appropriate to talk of academics. I had made the trek by bus from Kansas City mainly to work on Spanish and do some serious studying, so I was there for school. I ended up taking two serious literature courses. The first dealt with the Picaresque Novel of Spain, a core course in Spain's Golden Age Literature. The lady who taught was top flight, her clear Spanish a "gift" to me as were her wonderful lectures. There were no exams but we were expected to write a lengthy paper based upon the reading of one of the many Picaresque novels. I, naïve once again, asked the scholarly lady, "Which is the best?" ["Cuál es la mejor?"]. So I naively chose to read "Guzmán de Alfarache," perhaps the longest and most difficult of them all, over one thousand pages of Baroque era Castillian Spanish. I should have chosen "Lazarillo de Tormes," a far shorter novel but one no less appreciated by those in the know. Many an hour was spent trying to get through the Aguilar leather bound edition with dictionary in hand and then write the paper.

The second course was equally good and demanding. Its subject matter was the "Prose of Cervantes other than the 'Quixote.'" This was no small matter considering Cervantes wrote the many "Exemplary Novels," Pastoral Novels and the like. The "Exemplary Novels" in particular are considered small "jewels" in his astounding total work. The professor, Mexican by nationality, comported himself more like an English Don, with good reason since he was an Oxford Man. Thus whether for his own practice or our edification the entire course was dictated in high "King's English." So why was I in Mexico? Be calm. Indeed all the difficult readings in 16th and 17th century Spanish prose were demanding enough and improved my Spanish. But I think the Don improved my English or at least gave me a greater appreciation of it. (A similar event would happen just a year or two later with Professor Edward Sarmiento, mentor at Saint Louis University who taught as well in the King's English.)

Monday, July 23. I wrote: "Sick of school, sick, sick, sick!" I started writing one of the papers for school that afternoon. "There was another cultural moment at the university: Last Friday Agustín Yañez visited one of the classes. He was famous for his novel "At the Edge of the Water "["Al Filo del Água,"] an important "Novela de la Revolución." There was time for discussion and questions. Since I had not read any of his stuff, the visit left a little to be desired. He was distinguished with suit and tie, a bit elderly, but his Spanish was easy enough to understand. One has to be a true student of Mexican literature to appreciate the moment."

"Last night. We were at Garibaldi Square again with mariachis all over the place. Drinks and dancing at the Tenampa! The party girls were there and available! Curran was shocked when we first sat down and my sweetie dance partner was fondling ever so delicately my crotch! First time for everything! From the Tenampa we moved on to "México Típico." More drinks — tequila con sal y limón. Quite a night. We danced, drank, spent time outside with the mariachis, all singing Mexican favorites and arrived home late. We did not take the girls up on their offers, a good thing in retrospect.

"Sunday. What can I say? I was at home studying. Monday: I missed the "pesero" on Avenida Insurgentes to school so took the bus; the minstrels were on the bus on the return.

Tuesday, Wednesday; school.

"Thursday. Another Mexican Cultural Moment. We went to the Estadio Azteza of the UNAM to see a major soccer game, Necaxa versus Oro. We ended up accidentally seated next to the manager of a team from Texcoco who graciously and patiently explained much of what was going on to me. The stadium is huge, holds some 70,000 (this was before my Rio de Janeiro days and Maracanã), and was about two thirds full that night. The outside is decorated with volcanic rock and Aztec motifs; the shape is oval. Some highlights: those in the upper deck wadded up newspapers, set them afire and threw them down on us in the lower deck. We were fortunately far enough under the top deck so that we were out of the way; others were not so fortunate." I wrote: "The game was really good. Two black Brasileños played for Oro and were good and fast. The game started lopsidedly as Oro made two goals in the first ten minutes. At half time it was sprinkling rain. The final score was Oro 4, Necaxa 3." We took the trolley home (35 centavos) and noticed the street urchins ["gamines"] who jumped on the back to ride free—a dangerous undertaking.

"Friday. I was back to the movies with Larry Older and Ron Richards where we saw "Duel in the Sun" with Gregory Peck, an oater. The movie theater was gorgeous, a "Rococó" type palace. Afterwards we ate at an Italian Restaurant on Niza and then repaired to "Gitanerias", a famous night club in Mexico City. The floor show consisted in songs from diverse regions of Spain, flamenco dancers with castanets, dramatic readings, and then more dancers and singers. The highlight for me was when the famous Mexican guitarist David Moreno played "Malagueña" and more.

An aside: contrasting the differences between television in the U.S. and Mexico. One of the most popular programs during my stay in Mexico City was a 30 minute program contrasting four styles of Spanish guitar by the best musicians in the country: classic, flamenco, Mexico and romantic guitar. It only whetted my appetite for the instrument and the music. I am positive no such program ever existed in the U.S. One of my "bucket list" items yet today is the guitar festival held each March in Guanajuato! "We then walked to the Paseo and to the Hotel María Isabel, Mexico's newest and snazziest, went to the top floor with the bar and listened to jazz. Very elegant, very expensive."

"Saturday. Carlos, Ricardo and I went again to "Variedades" in the Teatro Latino, the show with actress Silvia Raynal.

"Sunday. There was another "miss" with Eduardo Matheu's friend. Alberto's car broke down, or so he said, so we could not make it to visit his ranch. "About like the bad luck I've been having." We have plans to go to the "Hipódromo" for horse racing. "Time will tell." I never really did make connection with Silva; there were lots of excuses, a learning experience for me. I salvaged that day however by going to a French movie and ate at the Pizza Real that night.

"Monday. Curran cut classes and went to the Guatemalan Consulate to get the visa for the coming trip.

"To Teatro Blanquita. The major Mexican stars appear in "Variedades." There were singers, the star the "blond" Silvia Pinal, dancers, an "Entrevista con Chucho Herrera," ventriloquists, other comedians, a steel drum band from Trinidad and the Limbo. There was a long walk home that night via the downtown; I recall walking past the "Monumento de la Revolución.""

"Wednesday. Finished classes. Hurrah! I think the grades were good but won't know for a while." An aside from school that summer: There was a glass partition between the building of our summer school and the other "regular" part of the university. At class dismissal times all the Mexican guys would gather to ogle the "gringas." I swear I saw steam on the window! I also recall the cafeteria where we drank coke, ate Mexican sandwiches ["tortas,"] and also recall the Mosaic Library of the UNAM (my note says "Juan O'Gorman." Was this the architect?) All seems foggy to me now. It was foggy to me then too.

9. Acapulco and the Sea

"About this time I made a momentous decision when I decided to go to Acapulco. We traveled in the luxury Oro Bus for 49 pesos with a stewardess, air conditioning, and bathroom, the works! This was "upper end" Mexico bus travel in 1962! I could only recall the much different bus trip from Laredo to Mexico City a few months earlier. We traveled overnight and I about froze from the more than efficient air conditioning system. Fortunately there was the distraction of the company of three American girls the entire way. It was raining when we reached Acapulco and I can remember the intense change in atmosphere with tropical warmth and humidity after the relative dryness of Mexico City at 7500 feet.

"We arrived shortly after dawn and the view of the ocean through the tropical hills, palm trees and all was something! It was the first time I had seen the ocean, any ocean! It was sheer beauty to me. I later would relive such memories in a reading of one of Carlos Fuentes' novels with his description of the high life of the Mexican upper class of the late 1950s in Acapulco by the sea.

"I spent the remainder of the first night in a cheap motel with a plethora of cockroach tourists, no air conditioning, etc. for 25 pesos a night (recall the exchange rate was still 12 to the dollar). There were mosquitoes, no towels, no soap; the place was a tropical beauty! I moved from there later that same morning to a moderate but clean place about two blocks from the beach. I was swimming on Caletilla Beach later the same day. It is difficult to describe my feelings at age 20 on this the first time I had seen the ocean.

Puerto Marquéz and the Bay of Acapulco

"It was wonderful. I swam until about 11:00 a.m. and then took a launch to Puerto Marquéz for 8 pesos. The trip took one hour counting the times the motor stopped in the small 4 passenger motor launch. The ride gave us a wonderful view of the entire Acapulco Beach Area, especially Caleta-Caletilla, Playa de Hornos, and Condesa. It was my first ride on the sea, and although it was not rough, the little boat rocked quite a bit. I guess we were still in Acapulco Bay. We had to wade ashore at Puerto Marquéz. I sat awhile and then listened to a blind man singing ballads. Then I went swimming; the waves were much stronger than on the beach in Acapulco proper, and there were many fewer people. There fortunately were beach hammocks available in the shade where you could relax without fear of getting sunburned (or so I thought). On the return trip we saw the "Virgen de la Bahía," an image 8 to 10 feet beneath the water; some kind of local legend was spouted about how it got there. We arrived safely back to the mainland about 4 p.m.

"Back at the hotel I showered, slept awhile in fact until about 1:30 a.m. There were some American girls about at the time so we all went swimming and ate until about 4 a.m.

"Next day I got up and walked all the way down Playa Hornos where I just sat and watched the ocean and the sea gulls for a couple of hours. Remember it was the first time at the ocean. Then I took a city bus back to the hotel. The bus took some side streets off the main tourist drag and there one sees a very different Acapulco. It was very poor, a bit depressing, and as bad as anywhere I've seen in Mexico.

"Later I made my way back to Caleta Beach where I swam all afternoon. Then I ate at the São Paulo Restaurant and then went up to the famous "Quebrada" where I watched the sunset ["puesta del sol]," a marvelous sight, "one of the most beautiful sights I had seen up to then in my entire life." I met two girls from Mexico City; we talked, walked about and saw the cliff divers do their show. They dive from a cliff about 110 feet above the water, and the water is located in a strait between two cliffs with waves crashing on the rocks far below. The depth of the water is not sufficient to dive into until the waves come in, so there is much waiting, creating much drama and suspense. After each dive they climb up the rocky, craggy surface of the cliff to prepare to dive again. I found this rock climbing as exciting as the dives themselves. Legend has it that they pray to the Virgin for safety before they take the plunge. There is a little ceremony and much crossing of themselves beforehand.

"It was raining like crazy the following morning when I was set to depart for Mexico City, so I took a cab to the bus station and left the city by the sea. This bus ride would be more like Buñuel's famous movie "Mexican Bus Ride." This time it was a bad bus: the air conditioning did not work. I was seated immediately above the wheel well, the roughest place to ride and also could not stretch out. We had to stop various times to wait for cattle and burros to get out of the road. I recall going through Chilpancingo on the return trip.

Mark J. Curran

Here from the old notes is my take on Acapulco. "Acapulco is beautiful! I would enjoy spending more time there but I have one major complaint: you cannot go anywhere without someone having their hand out. On the beach you rent your chair, and buy "refrescos," [soda pop] plus tip. Then you tip the person getting you a taxi and the taxi driver himself. (Curran, farmer boy, welcome to the world.) But all in all it was a good experience."

10. Return to D.F.

"On the Sunday after the return Carlos, Ricardo and I went to the famous bull fight ["corrida de toros,"] the first time for me. I enjoyed the music very much — the "paso dobles" by the corrida band. It was impossible to take photos for it was overcast and rained later. There was much confusion about the seat assignment; we had to move once. "Makes me madder than hell because they all expect tips and still cannot do their job right." Curran: welcome to Mexico. I think the whole experience was beginning to wear on me a bit! I was going to buy a rain coat at the "corrida," but they wanted 20 pesos.

"The entry of the 'matadors' and their crew was impressive, but as I write I can't recall the name for it in Spanish. That was the end of anything impressive to me. The only exciting thing after the entry was when the bulls jumped the wooden barrier around the arena ["barrera"]; I counted at least seven times. The cape men were the best of the bunch, but that is not saying much. The "picadors" made me sick, the "bandilleros" were cowards, and the "matadors" or "toreros" were terrible! Each was allowed three "estocadas" for the kill, and nary a one could get the job done. They lost their capes several times, and the banderillas sometimes stuck and sometimes not. After the third bull I left; it had started to rain and I had seen all I wanted. It turns out the reason the "corrida" was not so good that day was that the "toreros" were "novilleros" or novices, and bad novices at that. I evidently was not alone in my feelings because a lot of other people, not just tourists, had left too. I'm glad I went, but I really did not care for it. Our rodeos have them beat a mile!

As I read this, once again, I believe I protest too much. And I hate to say it, but it sounds like the perspective of a typical gringo tourist, and I did not consider myself "typical." Summer was getting on and I believe the gringo was getting weary and a bit too testy. But a chance of pace with an incredible new experience would better my point of view.

However still thinking of the bull fights, an interesting perspective came years later, in 1968. I had the opportunity to see the truly famous Spanish "torero" "El Cordobés" in Nogales, Sonora, in a small bull ring but jammed with an enthusiastic crowd. He was on a well-paid circuit of all the major cities along the U.S.-Mexico border. I do not know how many "pases" he made that day on his knees, back facing the bull. See the well-written book "Or I'll Bury You in Mourning" to see his place in the annals of fine toreros in Spain.

Once again, these commentaries are a "gas." Mister naïve gringo, please step forward. I was only 19 and still had hay seed coming out of my ears.

B.   MEXICO TO GUATEMALA, AUGUST, 1962

The next day I would leave Mexico City by bus on an unforgettable first trip to Guatemala where I would rendezvous with friend Eduardo Matheu from Rockhurst, a native of Guatemala and my guide for the few days of my first visit to that incredible country.

1. The Bus Ride

"We left Mexico City on what would become a 35 hour bus ride from Mexico to Guatemala via the San Cristóbal Colón Line at 9:00 a.m. on a Thursday morning. We passed through Puebla first; the main street was very modern and nice. The beautiful churches of Puebla could be seen off in the distance from the highway, many with ornate mosaic domes and spires. Otherwise, the parts of town along the road all appeared the same as the regular small rural Mexican towns. The bus rode like hell and had neither muffler nor air-conditioning. From Puebla we passed through several smaller towns—Matamoros, Acatlán—and stopped to eat at the latter. The town was "typical" with row houses close to the street and almost no sidewalk. There were many beggars and vendors at the bus stop to meet you.

"From Puebla on south the landscape was pure hills and small mountains with cactus alongside. The road was winding all the way, almost to the point of making me car sick, the only time in my life (up to that time) I ever recall such an experience. Almost an hour before Oaxaca the mountains grew taller, the landscape greener; it all looked much more like Colorado with its pine trees. There was also much more water, more streams and rivers. We arrived in Oaxaca at 8 p.m., a very thriving tourist town because of its own beauty (which Keah and I would see years later) and the ruins of Monte Albán of Zapotec fame nearby.

"It was much warmer and I felt like I was in the tropics again. From there we traveled at night, so I have no idea of things except that the road was constantly winding and semi-mountainous. Next morning at dawn we arrived at Tuxtla Gutiérrez. There was a tire change which caused about an hour's delay; it was the hottest place I can recall on the trip, very humid, very wet but very beautiful.

"Tuxtla Gutiérrez was a very pretty little town up in the mountains. The roads were full of livestock, cattle and burros, and we passed many, many Indians along the side of the road, most of them dressed in the local, colorful weavings. Men as well as women wore skirts, hats of straw with flat brims (the hats reminded the gringo a bit of the old straw hat worn by the vaudeville hoofers). My lasting memory was that it was absolutely beautiful, the most impressive sight I had seen thus far on my first trip south of the border. One could contrast these present sights with the literally hundreds of miles of semi-desert terrain all the way south from Laredo to Mexico City.

2.   The Border

"We arrived at Ciudad Cuautémoc, the Mexican customs ["aduana"] before the Guatemalan frontier. There they took our Mexican tourist cards before we continued a bit farther to the Guatemalan border. There was revision of documents and luggage at a place called "La Mesilla." It was picturesque, at the foot of some magnificent mountains. There we climbed aboard for our bus trip to Quetzaltenango in northwest Guatemala. Here was where the real fun began.

"Later on, Eduardo Matheu's father would marvel at my trip through the Mesilla and the mountains, one of the most rugged routes possible in those times, but also one of the most beautiful." Years later when teaching summer school at the Universidad Francisco Marroquín in Guatemala City, my students would arrive in Guatemala by the "other" route, a train along the coast and the lowlands, this after been pick pocketed on the train.

"The bus was the equivalent of the sort of bus I used to ride to school in as a child in Kansas, except smaller; there were small, absolutely straight backed seats with no padding, no leg room whatsoever (at least for non-Mayan riders), and riding very hard. I believe they pulled some farmer out of the hills to drive. He wore no "uniform" as they did in Mexico. We went through about six miles of very pretty country before stopping to pick up about six Indians who totally overcrowded the bus. It was hot as we started on a trip I shall never forget.

"The road was either packed clay or gravel, truly the roughest road I had ever been on up to that point in my life (Brazil and Colombia would come later). It curved around mountains following the course of a river, getting uncomfortably close to the edge many times. The road was washed by recent rains and we came very close to going over the edge several times. This is not fantasy; it happens all the time in Latin America. (In 1975 Keah and I would experience very similar roads along the three chains of the Andes in Colombia and our host Mr. Emery was killed traveling from the lowlands to Bogotá on such a road just a few months later. He was hit head-on around a blind curve by either a bus or truck.) At times we were on a ledge, far above the river, so an accident would surely have been fatal. And a brief note: perhaps to save the battery, drivers on all vehicles at night would only put on their lights at curves.

"All this time one of the natives was talking a mile a minute in a very loud voice, disturbing, I gather, not just me. Fortunately he got off a bit up the road. We stopped at a little shack for lunch and I was glad later I had decided to not eat anything. I did buy some oranges and peanuts to get by on from some vendors (one cent apiece for the oranges). About ten miles up the road from the lunch stop a little boy vomited all over the bus, including on some passengers. I was just out of range of the vomit, but not the stench which remained with us the rest of the trip. Fortunately we could keep the windows open or there would have been more vomiting.

"We then stopped at Huehuetenango for another meal which I also skipped. At that point the bus driver informed me I had to buy another ticket, that the line did not accept the one I had purchased in Mexico City (one way to Guatemala), but I insisted it was good and refused to pay. Keep in mind I was the only gringo on the bus. He did convince some passengers to pay more; at the border they had charged for revision of passports and luggage, possibly a method to augment the miserable salaries of border guards and/or inspectors. Welcome to the land of the bribe ["mordida"].

"From then on we really got up into the mountains. Flashback to "la Mesilla": a vivid memory was of the small cornfields ["milpas"] literally climbing the side of the hills. The common joke in Guatemala is the one about the Indian who got drunk and fell out of his cornfield! Now the ride was staggeringly beautiful—lush green, tropical. "I would someday like to make the trip again," I wrote then. Later I added, "Not likely now since Guatemala is now militarized due to the conflicts in Central America." The last comment must be from the late 1970s.

"As I said, we climbed considerably, now in high mountains, but we had left the course of the river, so it was not so frightening . . . at first! The road itself was badly washed, more so than the one to Huehuetenango, debatable to call it a road at all. The scenery was pretty, more expansive, but I did not notice details so much because of the terrible bumpy ride. Two times we ran into places in the road I would have never attempted to cross. The driver stopped the bus, got out, took a look, and then plunged through. The worst place in the road, and I thought we were going over the edge for sure, was high, high up in the mountains along a scarcely recognizable path. From there it got worse!

"At approximately the highest point on the trip, in the mountains outside Quetzaltenango, we had a flat tire. We all piled out of the bus while they fixed it; the temperature could not have been much over 40 degrees Fahrenheit. But from there on we made it without further incident to Quetzaltenango. The ride obviously is etched in my memory yet today. And as I re-write this, I would love to see that part of the world again. Will it be so?

3. Quetzaltenango, a Reunion with Eduardo Matheu and Highlights of Guatemala

Mark and Eduardo Matheu, Quetzaltenango, Guatemala

"In Quetzaltenango I waited for Eduardo Matheu my friend from Rockhurst Days who arrived at 7 p.m. We had a good meal, drove around town some, but by the time we got back to the hotel it was dark and late. They said they had no rooms so we ended up sleeping in the car. Next morning Eduardo took care of some business for his family's pharmaceutical factory, a booth at the fair ["feria"] being set up for Independence Day Celebration, and then we took off for Lake Atitlán. We passed through very high country with large lots of wheat being raised on the slopes, as well as barley; there also were many sheep. We passed through one Indian village that was particularly interesting: it was market day and the roads were filled with the locals. Here you could see the poverty of Guatemala. We passed through a plateau at almost 11,000 feet, the wheat growing area, but the crops were very thin at that altitude.

4. Lake Atitlán [Lago de Atitlán]

Lake Atitlán, Later Days.

Lake Atitlán impressed me as one of the most beautiful places I had ever seen. It still does to this day; witness hundreds of slides taken over the years. It is surrounded by mountains, volcanoes, and the water level itself is at about 7000 feet. There is a beautiful waterfall on the way down from the top to the town of Sololá, this via a winding road through lush tropical foliage. Memory is a bit fuzzy, but I believe the Lake is surrounded by twelve villages, each with descendants of the Mayas. Each village maintains its local customs and way of dress, a very complicated matter the latter. Men's styles with perhaps a straw hat, a heavy woven wool black jacket with a bat on the back, a sort of woven skirt, and rough leather sandals were no match for the intricate, beautiful woven blouses ["huipiles"], skirts and headdresses of the ladies (and their daughters matched them). The villages were named after Catholic saints and a small parish church was at the center of each village along with the local "pila" or water fountain. Keah and I would visit these villages time and again in later years. On one visit we saw the remains of shattered buildings from the earthquake of 1976, and everyone, rich and poor, lived in houses with tin roofs replacing the heavy tiles which had killed many in the quakes. In one church in San Antonio de Palopó, the poor interior was with cracked ceiling and walls, the altar removed, but rows of statues of saints were stacked along the walls, many of the saints in local Indian dress. The volcanoes surrounding Atitlán stood high

85

as sentinels guarding this sacred place (for it was a sacred place in Pre-Colombian Mayan history), the water of the lake then was clear, icy cold with a healthy population of fish to supplement the natives' diet and the steep slopes along the lake were rich volcanic soil fit for cultivation of diverse vegetables. We would hike many times in later years to the diverse villages or take a canoe across the lake to a market where one outstanding crop was that of huge avocados!

"Eduardo and I first went for a boat ride on the lake, the water crystal clear and cold. The lake is extremely deep, and in fact they claim to never have found the bottom. They suspect there is an underground river which empties closer to the west and the Pacific. The water is in fact almost icy, very cold to swim in. Eduardo and friends would use wet suits, snorkel and fins to dive in later years. The Indians in the twelve villages surrounding the lake have dugout canoes they use for transportation as well as for fishing. There are many kinds of fish in the lake (c. 1962); at this time many black bass abound for good sport fishing. Most famous are the weavings of the villages surrounding the lakes.

La Casa Contenta Hotel, Later Days, Keah

"After the boat ride we went to the Matheu cabin on the lake, a cabin which in fact belonged to an aunt of Eduardo's. His father would build only years later after literally negotiating for years with Indians to purchase the lot. We fixed chile and hot dogs at the cabin. Then we went to the major tourist Hotel at that time—la Casa Contenta—and swam. We met other kids at the hotel ("ladinos" or Hispanic middle and upper class ones to be sure) and played "mosca." That night we went to the Hotel Casa Contenta, ate a wonderful steak dinner, drank and danced to marimba music with the young ladies of social class whose families came to the lake each weekend. We later went o Eduardo's uncle's lodge where we drank Johnny Walker Red, my introduction to drinking Scotch whiskey, and talked until late in the evening or a.m. This is the uncle with the fishing fleet out of Puerto San José on the Pacific Coast.

"The next morning we got up at 5:30 a.m. and went out in the boat to fish for black bass. We used spinning rods with minnows as bait. Eduardo's father and others caught eight nice bass (the week before they had caught 28). If I had known then how to handle a García-Mitchell spinning outfit like I do now, I would have caught some too, but I did not and just got tangled. Back at Panajachel, the town by the lake, we went to the native market, bought bananas, bread, avocados, and cooked the fish for a royal meal. We slept for a while and then headed for Guatemala City. There was ash rain on the way; one of the huge volcanoes was erupting.

5.   Arrival in Guatemala City [Ciudad de Guatemala]

"We arrived in Guatemala City at night, and a few miles outside the city we stopped to see the fire and lava flow of the volcano erupting in the distance. This was the first time I had seen a live volcano. We could not see the crater, but we could see the lava flow and smoke from the crater.

"We stopped and viewed Guatemala City from the high point of the Pan American Highway, a beautiful sight at night. Then we went immediately to Eduardo's house for dinner. I met his father, mother, and his brother Roberto and his wife. Roberto was later killed in an automobile accident in the late 1960s. Concha, or Conchita, his mother, was very sweet, always telling local stories and Indian legends. His father was very formal, straight-laced, and he demanded sport or suit coat and tie at the dinner table (which I borrowed from Eduardo).

An aside. You have to draw the line somewhere.

"Aside from the formality at the table, a memory or two are of interest. One meal was chicken, vegetables and all the trimmings, the chicken served in the usual manner, breast, legs, wings, thighs in pieces. The Matheus with napkin delicately in the lap ate the chicken European style—the fork in the left hand, the knife in the right, expertly dissecting the whole business. The farm boy watched, picked up the utensils as witnessed but simply could not achieve success. Finally I looked up and in a confessional mode admitted to one and all that starvation would come if I could not pick up the chicken with two hands and proceed "gringo" style. Being fine, gentle hosts they laughed (with me not at me) and encouraged me to finish the meal. Done and satisfied. I surmise there was some talk of the incident later, but never was I felt to be any the lesser.

Later events would mark Mark's success in Guatemala.

"But meal time always brought Mama Concha's tales. Here is one of Conchita's legends: the wife of Pedro Alvarado, the principal "conquistador" of Guatemala, an officer under Cortés in Mexico, is in mourning in his castle in old Antigua, with 12 ladies in waiting ["doncellas"]; then comes the flood from Volcán de Água overlooking the colonial capital of Antigua, then the earthquake. Indians live today where the castle was buried by the volcano; only the chapel is left. This is the same volcano that is erupting now, in 1962, near Antigua.

"Such tales, meant to be told to children for moral betterment, I guess, were fodder for laughter and jokes at the dinner table. I take it the family had heard them all a few times before.

"One other memory involved the national product, coffee. "Guatemaltecos" claim of course to have the best tasting coffee in the world, grown in incredibly rich soil in the shade of Jacaranda trees on the sides of the volcanoes. On the table was a small "creamer" but full of "esencia de café."

One added boiling water to the essence and whatever else you might want and thus the delicacy was savored." I agreed wholeheartedly at the time, but since then have had the "cafezinho" in Brazil the last 40 years, so perhaps a refresher course in Guatemala is in need.

"The next day, Eduardo and I visited Industria Farmacéutica (INFASA) owned by the Matheu family. The company was the largest in Central America at the time and manufactured many types of drugs for marketing throughout Central and South America. Eduardo's father was the head of the board but his oldest brother Julio was CEO at the time. I remember the antiseptically clean labs and production site and the offices. "Mejoral" a type of aspirin and pain killer was one of the principal products.

"After INFASA we visited an Indian market, and then went to the night clubs that night. I met Rodolfo Contreras (a student at Rockhurst along with Eduardo in my days there); his father was police chief of Guatemala in 1962. I recall Rodolfo as a privileged Latino at Rockhurst; I think he would agree. In 1962 he had a business going on the side: he was driving a big truck to the coast, buying oranges, and bringing them back to Guatemala City to sell. It was a bit difficult to fix the two images: playboy at Rockhurst—truck-driving capitalist in Guatemala!

Mayan Stela, Museum of Anthropology, Guatemala City

"The next day we went to the anthropological museum in Guatemala City to see Mayan relics and then to the National History Museum. That night we got dates and went to a nightclub. Next day there was a movie (Cantinflas—"Señor Ministro") with a plot like the "Secretário de Amantes" in the markets of Brazil, but this time in the Zócalo in Mexico City. Cantinflas would sit with his battered old typewriter in the plaza of the Zócalo and write love letters for the peasants in the city, folks who did not know how to read or write but still could fall in love and want to propose to a future wife. Of course Cantinflas' legendary double entendres and double talk were hilarious. After the movie there was bar hopping that night ending at the Morocco Club. And the next day we visited Rodolfo's farm ["finca"].

"That night was Pablo's birthday. Pablo was another brother of Eduardo's, a member of Opus Dei and with a hobby whose goal was to climb all the volcanoes of Guatemala, a long list. So all the family came to the house. I played guitar and sang for all, and we also went to another party that night. After the party we repaired to Club Morocco and then were stopped by the Guatemalan police with Eduardo having to make explanations at the station.

"The next morning I actually had an interview with Julio, Eduardo's oldest brother who is CEO of INFASA. Recall that my major in undergraduate school was Business Management with a Minor in Spanish and the nebulous goal of working in Latin America. Evidently the series of factors of my facility in Spanish, love for Latin America and Latinos, some guitar playing and mainly the friendship with Eduardo along with some rational answers to Julio's questions brought an offer for a job at INFASA. What Julio explained was that they needed someone proficient in both English and Spanish, the first to deal with chemical suppliers from the United States, the second to help expand their market in Central America. I was offered a modest entry salary and expenses for living in Guatemala; the rest was a bit vague at that point, but it was understood I would begin after receiving the B.S.B.A from Rockhurst, along with Eduardo, in 1963.

These are the moments in life that determine an entire future. What would happen is that I would return to Rockhurst, weigh carefully the offer, but ultimately decide to pursue graduate studies in language and culture in Latin American Studies at Saint Louis University. It was a happy decision. But many times over the years I would wonder "What if?" Honestly, today I doubt I would have been able to acculturate to Guatemala, this in spite of all the positive points, and I doubt even more that I would have been a success in the business. It never happened so we are dealing with pure conjecture.

6. The Farm. [La Finca –Vista Bella y el Molino]

Mark, Wheat Field, Matheu' Farm, Guatemala

"Friday. Eduardo and I motored to Eduardo's family farm that p.m. There was heavy rain and we had to go through the Indian village of Tecpán via a back road to get to the farm. We arrived at the Molino Vecino (or was it Venécia?); there was a fire in the fireplace in what seemed to me to be a beautiful country type lodge; we ate and to bed. "There was a gorgeous, clear stream running through the middle of the farm; I fell in love with this place." It is necessary to explain that growing up in central Kansas, there are no clear streams. Only in later days in Colorado and now in Guatemala would I see such beautiful scenes. I would visit the farm again alone in 1969 and then with Keah in later years and even after the major earthquake in 1976. Eduardo would add orchards and even apples named after him to the green alfalfa and wheat fields and other cultivations.

"I thought I had arrived in agricultural heaven at the "finca." Next morning we rode horse back to the nearby Mayan Quiché ruins of Ixché. Not only was it beautiful but we were the only ones there.

"The farm is beautiful with the house by the stream (thus the Molino) with a lot of clear space next to it, pine trees, green grass, much like Colorado. There is a little dam in a beautiful green valley which controls the flow of water to the farm, of course notwithstanding tropical rainfall as well. One of the main crops was wheat, familiar to the Kansan, alfalfa, but many other crops. Mayan villages surrounded the farm, and in fact the Arbenz Regime of the early 1950s would establish a land reform policy which would take a good share of the acreage for distribution to the natives.

7.   Other Travels and Sights in Guatemala

Mark, Canoe-Taxi, Mayan Owner, Lake Atitlán

"We left that night for a return visit to Lake Atitlán and another visit to Casa Contenta, the old traditional hotel by the lake, than to El Rancho Grande, a German Hostel where I would stay with Keah years later. The next day we swam in the lake's icy water, went boat riding and returned to Guatemala City via the old road with beautiful scenery, driving around the back side of the lake in the midst of pine forest.

Eduardo, Mother Superior, Santa Clara Convent, Antigua, Guatemala

"Monday. Eduardo and I got our travel papers for the return trip to Mexico and home to Abilene. That afternoon we drove to Antigua, saw the lava flow from the Volcán de Fuego, and met Eduardo's aunt who is the mother superior of an order of nuns at one of the famous, old convents. I can't recall which order or convent, maybe the "Capuchinas" or Santa Clara. We then went to see the ruins of the Capuchin monastery and the old church dating from 1573! Both were destroyed by the earthquake of "Volcán del Água." It took 200 years to build the church and after only 17 years of use it was destroyed.

Eduardo, Mark, the Pacific Ocean, Puerto San José, Guatemala

"Tuesday. We went to the pueblo San José on the Pacific. The terrain goes from mountains to flat, wet country near the ocean where they grow cotton, sugar cane, bananas and raise cattle. Puerto San José was poor and seemed very backward to me; we went to the ship dock where Eduardo's uncle has a fishery. One of the big ships went aground the day before (there is no natural bay or port). They were unloading it and stripping it of anything of value. Otherwise, it was beyond use.

"We swam there; the ocean was very rough with much bigger waves than at Acapulco. The sand is black, the result of volcanic activity. You can only go about ten meters into the water because there is an undertow. The reason the sea is so rough is that it is indeed open sea; there is no natural bay like Acapulco. We had a lunch of raw oysters, água de coco, and later found a restaurant where we had a good serving of shrimp for about 75 cents U.S. We swam in the ocean and returned (I recall how the black sand burned your feet!)

"That night we returned to Guatemala City and attended the 15th anniversary party of the Granai-Townson Compañia de Seguros. (My original classic guitar music folder was a souvenir from that night.) There was an excellent Guatemala marimba band, excellent food, scotch ran free; all of us drank too much. A friend brought me home; I had to scale the wall to get in. Eduardo was stopped once again by the Guatemalan police on the way home and his car was confiscated. After much to-do, it was all straightened out eventually. His father did seem a bit upset about it all. Young men and their shenanigans in Guatemala!

"The next day We had dinner at Pío Castañeda's house, went to the market in the p.m. for souvenirs, and that night a party at Eduardo's aunt's house with mariachis. I played some music. It was big party time. Does the reader see why I liked Guatemala?

8. Back to Mexico City

Ricardo, Eduardo, Mark and Carlos, "La Tenampa," Plaza de Garibaldi, Mexico City

"Eduardo and I eventually flew back to Mexico City, had a reunion with Carlos Maravilllos, his cousin Ricardo and celebrated my 21st birthday in Garibaldi Plaza with all the girls. It was a wild night on the town in Mexico with diverse houses of prostitution, palaces, and finally home. I am permitted to say however that Mark's virtue was preserved, principally from drinking too much and the care of friends.

9.   Home to the U.S.A., Abilene, and the Return to Rockhurst

"After the wild night at the Tenampa, we said goodbye to my wonderful hosts and friends the Maravillos, and Eduardo and I went by bus all the way to Kansas City. Then Eduardo came home with me to Abilene, thoroughly enjoyed my family, my home and my parents. I can only recall a long bus ride from Mexico City, flirting with girls and drinking rum on the bus. Such were the days of college and my first trip to Guatemala.

All was new and I wrote these observations, in retrospect, in 1985: "Not only was the country absolutely gorgeous, all new and exciting to me, and of course politically safe, long before the turbulent late 1970s and 1980s, but the real difference was in having a friend there and being shown the country as I was. I do not believe I have ever enjoyed such hospitality and good fortune in travels again."

Later days with friends Jim Emery in Colombia, and Flavio Veloso, Jaime Coelho and Henrique Kerti in Brazil, would modify this observation. "Certainly it was the most absolutely wonderful introduction possible to Latin America and determined my enthusiasm and future joy for it."

Addendum: The friendship with Eduard Matheu prospered. I would see him again in Guatemala in 1969, in 1970 with Keah, in 1976 and 1977 when I directed ASU's Summer School in Guatemala and in California with Eduardo's future wife, son Harry and his schooling at UCAL Irvine in tropical agriculture.

Addendum 2: I cannot begin to say how this trip changed my life. A humble hayseed from Kansas was exposed to the absolute beauty of Mexico and Guatemala. I would dedicate the rest of my adult professional life to Latin America, the Spanish and Portuguese Languages and cultures and wonderful times there. The decision to not take the job offered to me by Eduardo's brother Julio at INFASA, but rather to pursue a Ph.D. in Spanish and Latin American Studies at Saint Louis University in 1966 would change the course of my life. But these memories are indelible and a joy to me yet today.

Mark J. Curran

SENIOR YEAR AT ROCKHURST 1962-1963

My roommate for senior year was Tim Braithwaite; we lived in the new dormitory which was much like the older ones on the south side of campus. Tim and I got along well. He would have a very successful career in the Department of Defense developing the use of computers and would go on to write many important books on Business Management and the use of computers. He and his girlfriend Kathy whom he later married would visit us in Tempe years later. It was Tim, through Kathy, who would introduce me to Ellen Hart whom I dated most of our senior year and took to that all important Junior-Senior Prom at a country club in North Kansas City in the spring of 1963.

I continued good relations and friendships with the Latinos at Rockhurst.

That fall of senior year, 1962, I decided to apply for graduate school in Spanish and Latin American Studies. I sent applications to the top schools in the USA with that specialty, was accepted by Stanford with a TA but no fellowship, LSU, Tulane, etc. but accepted an NDEA Fellowship to Saint Louis University. There were reasons: I was recommended at Saint Louis by friend and mentor Vernon Long of Rockhurst Spanish days. Vernon in fact would leave Rockhurst my senior year to pursue his own Ph.D. in exactly the same program at Saint Louis, and it was he who so highly recommended me to Father Rosario Mazza, S.J., Director of the Modern Language Department at Saint Louis University. I was so naïve yet about all this. It probably was a mistake to turn down Stanford, or at least try to negotiate the offer; I had no idea how to do such things. But I liked the Jesuits, Saint Louis offered just what I wanted—including Portuguese and Luso-Brazilian Studies, and I had some ties to friends in St. Louis, so the decision was made. Professor Long was with me my first year in St. Louis but left the program with coursework finished but not dissertation and took a job teaching at Otero Junior College in La Junta, Colorado, a rather stark contrast to the big city.

I believe it was Spring, 1963, senior year at Rockhurst when I would go to St. Louis for the first time, staying with good friend Bill Bockelman of Rockhurst days and music days there. I had my first interview with Father Mazza, the director of the NDEA program at Saint Louis who gave me the frightening reading list for the Ph.D. and told me to brush up on my Latin as part of that list. He also wondered if I liked girls. I think he wondered if I was a "straight shooter" but who knows.

There was much less intensive studying senior year; I had already established a very high g.p.a. and had been accepted for graduate school and the grant at SLU. But there were some glitches. First among them was the fateful Business Law course required for the Business Management Major. It is worthwhile to repeat a bit of the story. It was taught by Brunswick Man Mr. Noonan. I had a D at mid-term, but needed a C to graduate because I was a business major. It was all very ironic: I had this terrific grade point average, in fact had "honors" in Business Management because I did well in most of the courses including marketing, accounting, and Problems in Management. I probably could have been a success at management, the day to day operations of a business. But I was a jerk in Business Law. The material was a total mystery to me and seemed to come from another planet. Good friend, former roommate Denny Noonan tutored me; he was whizzing through the course. He said, "Mark, it is all common sense." I was befuddled because the law was altered in each line of the text. The pressure was on; the outcome I can only speculate on at this point. I received a C after cramming and studying hour upon hour for the final. Did good Mr. Noonan offer me the "gift" or did I actually make the C? I can only say this: I am eternally grateful to him for passing me. And the memory of all this affected me greatly years later when I was a full-fledged college professor teaching Spanish at ASU in Tempe, Arizona. I realized that there were students in my Spanish language classes who were there because of a requirement, had absolutely no aptitude or desire for Spanish and were "sweating it out." My response: "Come to class, do the home work and we'll see." More important yet: a human being may be incredibly talented in a certain area and a dunce in another; who am I to keep that person from excelling in life?

And this of course recalls once again that fateful day before classes in 1959 when Dean Gough allowed me to change from Liberal Arts to the Business Major thus eliminating the requirements in higher math and science. The good Jesuit in effect did not keep me from excelling in my chosen field of language and culture and in professional life thereafter. So maybe there was more flexibility in the "Ratio Studiorum" that I thought.

SOCIAL LIFE SENIOR YEAR

I still worked at the language laboratory and had band jobs. I spent a lot of time with girlfriend Ellen and lots of time with the Latinos. There was a trip to the Ozarks in the spring with Tim, Kathy, Ellen, and there are memories of swimming, beer and fun. And there was the senior prom, a wonderful dance and party. I should say, although things might have moved on romantically with Ellen, my mind was set on the future, on graduate school and the goal of the future Ph.D. Happily, so I understand, Ellen had a "Plan B" as well and married another guy, I think in the armed forces.

Mark, Graduation, Rockhurst College, 1963

GRADUATION, MAY, 1963

It was a momentous and wonderful time. My parents came to campus for the ceremony. In a bit of an unusual hookup, they were together with Eduardo Matheu's parents at the same table for dinner. It was a very joyous occasion. Then we would all split for our future endeavors. It would only be years later when Eduardo and I would renew the friendship.

As I was set for the next three years and more in graduate school, there was less urgency for summer employment, but an interesting six weeks took place in Kansas City after graduation from Rockhurst. I was offered a post to teach English in the Rockhurst summer program and accepted the job. The salary was small but included room and board at the dormitory. I taught basic grammar and conversation to some twenty students, most from Latin America, but also with a smattering from Japan.

Time passed with work on campus with classes, but we had field trips which are of importance in this narrative. One outing was to the rather famous Kansas City Museum of Art near the Plaza; the claim to fame being Thomas Hart's many paintings of "America." But a second outing really is indelible in the memory.

President Harry Truman, from Missouri and as some said as stubborn as the Missouri Folkloric Mule, established his presidential library in Independence. Mr. Truman, still vibrant and active in 1959, would come to the museum to give short talks and appear to tourists. Our English study group had a planned outing to the museum one fine day. All went well, the students saw the exhibits, and we all convened in the auditorium in the p.m. for a short appearance of President Truman. Details are fuzzy as time has passed, but some indelible memories remain. The format was as follows: the President was at the podium, accepted a few questions and gave answers. All went swimmingly until one of my students, from Japan, rose, cleared his throat and asked why United States Troops were still in Okinawa, sixteen years after the end of World War II and the Atomic Bombs in Hiroshima and Nagasaki.

Truman, in effect, "lost it." He said, "You stupid Japanese sonofabitch, you &^%&*(&^^," or the like. I cannot recall his reasoning or his statements, but only the tone of the reaction. But he left no doubt as to his past decisions, the need for U.S. troops to remain in Okinawa, and also the great debt that the Japanese should have felt for help in reconstruction and defense yet from North Korea and China.

I mention this anecdote along with the text already concluded only to relive memories with Presidents Eisenhower, Kennedy and Truman up to that time in my young life. Not bad for a farm boy.

FINAL THOUGHTS

So the four years at the Jesuit undergraduate liberal arts school came to a close. Looking back, what can one expect other than memories of an 18 to 21 year old, naïve, kid. As we say in 2012, "It is what it is." The small town farm boy from Kansas went to the "big" city of Kansas City, Missouri, was exposed to the classic Jesuit program for boys of that age, and not only survived but excelled in certain areas. With a public school education in a small town in Kansas, with no previous Catholic education other than catechism by the nuns, it was a learning experience. Yet, as previously stated, being young, naïve and really "without a clue," the days passed, the courses were finished, the socializing and beer drinking were survived, the very limited dating with girls was concluded, but these memories remain. They are a portrait of the times. Time passed, I suspect we grew more in years than in wisdom (notwithstanding the college motto,) and for me the instruction in Spanish, the invaluable friendships with the Latinos and the practice in language they provided, the growth in music and the guitar, and especially that summer in Mexico and Guatemala in 1962 would mark the future.

But so did the Jesuits. It would only be years later, in Spain at Loyola, that much of my appreciation for them came to fruition. I would spend the next three years working on the Ph.D. at Saint Louis University, a story to be told in Part III of this book. Then a year was spent in Brazil doing research for the dissertation. Then there was a brief return to St. Louis with much travail to finish the dissertation, job interviews and a safe landing at Arizona State University in Tempe, Arizona, where I would spend my entire teaching career. But there would be a happy return to Rockhurst in the year 2000, a culminating experience at my first Jesuit School.

POST SCRIPT. THE ST. THOMAS MORE ACADEMY OF ALUMNI SCHOLARS.

Father Knierk, S.J., Dean, Rockhurst, Mark, St. Thomas More Academy of Alumni Scholars, Rockhurst College, 2000

Rockhurst College buddies Mark, Denny Noonan, Bill Bockelman

Sometime in early 2000 I received a call from the Alumni Office of now Rockhurst University. They informed me I had been chosen to receive an award for outstanding scholarship as an alumnus and thus would be invited to be part of the St. Thomas More Academy of Alumni Scholars. I am not sure how they came to know of my work, but I was invited to campus that beautiful fall for a meeting with the dignitaries and a fine dinner in old Massman Hall with speeches and my own emotional speech of acceptance. I was encouraged to invite a few friends, so my wife Keah and daughter Katie joined me as well as my sister Jo Anne and husband Paul Whitehair of Abilene and niece Lisa and her husband Drake who lived nearby. School chums who could make it were Bill Bockelman, Bill Rost and Denny Noonan. A wonderful time was had by all. Since that time additional books came out, in fact three major books on Brazil's folk—popular poetry and one, an autobiographic memory of growing up on the Kansas farm and accompanying school days in Abilene. So I feel not only honored and fortunate for the St. Thomas More Academy but believe my subsequent work more than "made the case" for the award. Perhaps I am most proud to be in the company of no less than Father Walter Ong, S.J. the great scholar of American Literature at Saint Louis University.

PART III.
THE JESUITS, SAINT LOUIS UNIVERSITY AND A FURTHER STEP IN COMING OF AGE

Overview, Saint Louis University Campus
Photo by Bradley Arteaga/ Courtesy of Saint Louis University, copyright 2011, SLU

Possibly a bit more mature, I would enter phase two of education with the Jesuits, this from the Fall of 1963 to summer of 1966. A year long stint in Brazil would follow, doing dissertation research for a Ph.D. in Spanish and Latin American Studies by virtue of a Fulbright Hays Grant; then there was a return to St. Louis and then Abilene to write the dissertation. Along the way came job applications and then the first and as it turns out only job at Arizona State University from 1968 to 2002 and retirement.

Life was much different as a serious graduate student with goals from which I never wavered. This is the continuation of that story.

1. How It Began

A bit of this is repeating the story from Rockhurst days. My mentor Vernon Long, to whom I owe so much, had suggested that for me to do anything serious in the field of Spanish I would have to have foreign language experience, thus the tale I have already told of the summer school in Mexico City at the National University and the subsequent trip to Guatemala. It was during the senior year at Rockhurst, with Vernon now absent himself as a student in the same NDEA program at Saint Louis University, that the future course was plotted.

My mentor suggested I apply for the NDEA Fellowship at Saint Louis University; this all took place in early fall, 1962. Actually I applied to what I knew then as the best programs in Spanish at diverse universities in the U.S. I applied to Tulane in New Orleans, Stanford and Saint Louis, among others. I actually received a fellowship for the Ph.D. at Stanford, was accepted, but at that time without a tuition scholarship. Through the good word of Vernon Long, I was accepted in the NDEA Fellowship program at Saint Louis University. The latter would pay all expenses, and my previous connection with the Jesuits and economics determined that course of action. Yet I have pondered the wisdom of all this. I later would learn that a degree from Stanford would open all doors, but did not realize that then. Economics prevailed. Life would have turned out totally different at Stanford: would have I "made the grade" there? I think so. I learned from a good friend from Stanford in later days, Timothy Wong, that they probably would have granted me tuition relief had I done well freshman year. I did not know that then. But Saint Louis University opened other doors to a good life—job, marriage, a wonderful daughter and satisfaction in life.

So it was that I accepted the grant from SLU, and the new adventure and life began.

It all started in the spring of 1963 with my first visit to St. Louis and an interview with Father Rosario Mazza, the head of the Modern Language Department. I alluded to this earlier in the narrative. I was hosted by good friend Bill Bockelman, colleague of the Continental All Stars Band at Rockhurst. I stayed with his family in Brentwood during that first visit. What wonderful hosts they were! Visits to Stan Musial and Biggie's Restaurant (Stan Musial was one of my great baseball heroes of the times), a visit to the still thriving Gaslight Square in St. Louis with a restaurant with the "singing waiters," and Broadway show tunes from South Pacific, "If I loved you, Some Enchanted Evening," all impressed me as to the possibilities of time in St. Louis.

The "introductory interview" with Father Mazza was eye opening and terrifying. The friendly but all business Jesuit quizzed me: how is your Latin? Do you like girls? And he introduced me to the reading list for the Ph.D. which would guide the Ph.D. program. He encouraged me to review my Latin, read the classics from Roman Literature, all this for openers. I do not recall much said about Spanish and Spanish literature itself. My Latin was not up to reading in the originals, but I did try to at least read some of the list in English Translation. The interview ended and he said "I'll see you in September." Did the clever Jesuit want to know if I was a party animal, would women distract me from the goal, or exactly what? I'll never know. I believe he simply wanted to know if I was a serious student. The future would answer that. So I returned to Rockhurst for spring term senior year and a lot of socializing along with some serious study which I've already related. The die was cast.

It is interesting to know about the program at SLU. The National Defense Education Act was promulgated in Washington out of fear: the Russians had sent up Sputnik in 1957 and the U.S. wanted to compete with them. Critical parts of the world and critical languages were to be learned and mastered to somehow or other help the nation forge ahead in this "brain race." Spanish speaking countries in South America and Portuguese Brazil were on the list. So we were to be formed and prepared for a career in teaching these critical languages on the college level. In retrospect, SLU and the government got their money's worth. I would form students in Spanish and Portuguese for 43 years as a college professor.

2. Arrival at Saint Louis University, Fall, 1963

Griesidieck Hall and the Quadrangle
Photo by Bradley Arteaga, Courtesy of Saint Louis University, Copyright 2011, SLU

I arrived with clothes, dictionaries, my trusty Smith-Corona typewriter, and Sears Roebuck classic guitar in the fall of 1963 to my dormitory, driving a well-used 1957 Ford car, blue and white and in much need of repair. The dormitory was an H formed configuration; in the middle the tall and spiffy and new Griesedieck Hall, a name I understand vaguely to be associated with St.Louis beer money. I lived in one of the old dorm rooms in the wings to the side. Memories are of a Spartan existence, bed, desk, closet, and window sills full of black coal dust each a.m. if you kept the windows open. This would be home for two of the three years at SLU.

Dorm life suited me; my job was to study and I did not either require or want apartment living off campus. Cafeteria meals sufficed, but the main social aspect of the dorm was the central lounge in Griesedieck Hall where I met the Latinos on campus, some of whom would become close friends. This was where I practiced Spanish, and listened to no end of anti-American bullshit from the privileged Latinos whose parents could afford private school tuition in the USA. The discussions and debates were good preparation for many forays to Latin America later on. You learned to defend

111

yourself and your country. Many of the Latinos were graduate students of Medicine; Saint Louis had a very respectable program in that area. There were the wealthy escapees from Fidel Castro's Cuba railing against Fidel, and the wealthy sons of presidents and vice-presidents from Panama, Nicaragua, Ecuador, and Bolivia. A good close friend would be Mario Santizo from Guatemala. We clicked right away; he was the son of a modest coffee grower father, product of the Jesuit High School in Belize, a serious student and friend. Mario would be a colleague in many of the graduate Spanish classes at SLU, a friend at parties and socializing, and later on in life, we would host his daughter Chacha at our house in Arizona where she did an internship in the area.

One day during my first semester at SLU, while hanging out in the big glass lobby of Griesidieck Hall before crossing the quadrangle for a class in old Dubourg Hall, one of the Latinos, a Panamanian, rushed up and shouted, "Did you hear the news? President Kennedy has been shot in Dallas!" This was November 22, 1963, a date many of us of my generation shall never forget! He was the quintessential Catholic hero of the times, the first Catholic elected president of the United States, young, handsome, with an optimistic eye for the future. I've already told in Part II of him and Jacqueline's visit to Mexico City in 1962, of the glamour and aura of the couple who represented the best of the United States of America. In particular for my interests and future, his plan for friendship and economic development for Latin America, a real partnership, "The Alliance for Progress" was important. We were in shock, there was anger and tears. The funeral was a nationally televised event. It seemed that the United States would truly enter a "downward spiral" in the ensuing years. Conspiracy theories as to his death, the acerbic relationship between Lyndon Johnson and the Kennedys, and of course in a few years the nightmare of Vietnam would be on the horizon. It seemed like an age of optimism, of idealism, of elegance was passing—the Camelot so painted by the press at the time. I suspect that the class I attended in the next few minutes, Latin American History with well-known writer and Professor John Bannon, was a fitting moment as well. I do know classes were not cancelled, even at a Jesuit University, but there was a pall of sadness throughout the campus.

3.   Academics and the Ph.D. Program

Because of 1957, Sputnik and the urgency of the times, the National Defense Education Act and subsequent fellowships followed a modified, new twist in American Academics. The idea was to prepare bright, young Americans in expertise in essentially important areas or countries of the world that might assist in the national defense effort. Latin America was one of those areas; after all, Fidel Castro was now an avowed Socialist, enemy of the United States after the Bay of Pigs fiasco and the Soviet Missile Crisis in Cuba was contained. It was thought and feared that Russia would extend its tentacles through Latin America via Cuba. So that is why the Spanish and Portuguese languages (Brazil with its threat of a peasant revolution modeled after Cuba) and the diverse Spanish speaking countries of Latin America and Brazil were deemed important. It was never explicitly stated what we graduates would do in careers to further the U.S. objective other than teaching, but only that we would have the expertise for those languages and area studies.

So in short the Ph.D. program was termed "Spanish and Latin American Studies." The major would be the Spanish language and its respective literatures in Spain the mother country and in diverse Latin nations. One minor would be "Latin American Area Studies" with courses in history, anthropology, and economics of Latin America. Another minor which was extremely important to me was "Luso-Brazilian Studies," that is, the study of the Portuguese Language and the literature and respective cultures of Portugal and Brazil. Advanced knowledge of Spanish and Portuguese was a given; if you did not have the skills you were expected to get them and quickly! My minor in Spanish at Rockhurst and real-world practice qualified me in that area. This was not the case in Portuguese, but there was an intense 10 hour, one year immersion course in Portuguese language to jump start us in that area. I dare say that if one has a solid basis in Spanish, an ability or "gift" for language, and is a native English speaker, that skill in Portuguese comes readily, if, and it is a big "if," one really works at it.

The Spanish and Spanish-American Literatures did not seem to me to be keenly related to expertise in the respective countries. I would have thought that history, political science, economics and the like would be the ticket. But that was NOT the essence of the program, notwithstanding the minor in Area Studies which I loved. So the Jesuits and lay professors of Spanish commenced to give us what I would call a "classical" preparation in Spanish linguistics and a rather intense reading of the major works of the respective literatures. In the end I actually specialized in Spanish Golden Age Literature, 16th and 17th centuries, thus studying the works of Cervantes, Lope de Vega, Calderón de la Barca, Garcilaso de la Vega, Luis de Góngora, and the others.

The time frame is important. Because of the urgency to "catch" the Russians, the program was highly accelerated. I think there were 60 hours of coursework, comprehensive exams, research and writing of the Ph.D. dissertation and defense of the same. All the course work was expected

Mark J. Curran

to be accomplished in three calendar years. I began fall of 1963 and actually finished the degree the summer of 1968, so there were five years in total. The NDEA fellowship paid all tuition and a stipend which was to be used for room, board, books and incidentals, about $200 per month. If you were frugal you could get by, which I did. But it was a no-nonsense program; we were being paid to study, and that was what we did. This was not an assistantship program, thus we were not expected to teach, do research for senior professors or the like. It fitted me like a glove.

I had no problem living in a rather austere dorm room for three years, eating cafeteria food, and living in an at-times "cloistered" atmosphere. These did not keep me from dating and dating seriously a couple of the coeds, something I'll comment on as we go along. But there were parameters: nothing, but nothing would distract me from the final goal—the Ph.D. The absence of apartment living and who knows what relationships might have come of that did not keep me from an active social life. Like Rockhurst days, from Sunday afternoon to class dismissal on Friday p.m., it was all business. I recall spending time in the library on Saturdays as well, but Friday and Saturday nights were for socializing, and we put heart and soul into that endeavor.

4. Classes, Professors, Some Boredom and More Excitement

It's been a long time but there are memories and impressions to recount. Was our program "typical" of graduate programs throughout the nation? Over the years I learned that Catholic education, even by the esteemed Jesuits, in the mind of much of the U.S. public played a definite second fiddle to that of secular institutions, in particular the Ivy League schools, and high ranked state schools, both on the east and west coasts. Berkeley and Stanford reigned in the West; Harvard, Columbia, Princeton and Yale in the East and I'm leaving out a lot. Notre Dame, academically and in sports, of course was "king of the hill" of the Catholic schools, and three or four good Jesuit schools followed, Saint Louis University among them. Otherwise, SLU would not have been a participant in the NDEA program. But I also learned while on a Fulbright-Hays graduate fellowship for dissertation research in Brazil that my graduate education and preparation allowed me to compete readily with the candidates from the aforementioned "uppity" schools.

I must digress on this point. I was spared the "Catholic ghetto" syndrome by virtue of growing up in a farm community with some twenty-seven Protestant denominations and one Catholic Church, and being blessed with an outstanding public high school in Abilene, Kansas. The "ghetto" mentality was occasionally present however at Rockhurst and at Saint Louis. After all, the stated goal of Jesuit schools primarily on the undergraduate level was above all to educate Catholic youth with a well-rounded Liberal Arts Education. It was also imperative to further the student in his faith and to live a productive life in the faith. Years after my times an important added component became important: Christian, social service. I think that my goals in teaching at a public university preparing students in language and culture for 43 years might be related to that a bit.

The Jesuits wore their black robes and the stiff white collar; mass and confession were still offered at the college church; there was a crucifix in each classroom, and maybe we started the class with a prayer. You really have to differentiate undergraduate and graduate programs. I must say this above all: Why did I pick Spanish and Portuguese, the respective cultures of Spain, Portugal and Latin America to be a life-long endeavor? In no small way it was because they were Catholic. And more important yet, for the next forty years I would specialize in Brazil's "literatura de cordel" in part because of its Catholic, religious vision.

Having digressed, let me recall professors and classes. The first year in residence filled some pre-requisites and offered introductory courses in the graduate program; the next two years really got into the "meat" of it and offered the truly interesting courses.

Mark J. Curran

I believe we were required to take no less than four classes in Spanish linguistics: phonetics, morphology and syntax, etc. The professor—appearance, personality, methodology, and demeanor—fit the stodgy bill. He would arrive in class with a stack of 3 X 5 note cards, copy the material to the blackboard, offer just a few comments and leave. The chalkboard thus contained page after page of etymologies from Latin to Spanish, etc. This was NOT my cup of tea. Colleague Dan Hayes, steeped in Latin, classical Greek and the like, knew it all and did not seem to mind. It never caught my interest; I learned some basics, retained less, but made decent grades and survived the ordeal. The professor was a kindly gentleman anyway.

On the other hand I was obsessed with Brazilian Portuguese and Brazil from the very beginning. The intensive first-year course was taught by a Brazilian, a Jesuit from Rio Grande do Sul in southern Brazil. Thus he spoke with the regional Brazilian Portuguese accent which trilled the initial R, the double R, and even the final R. I would learn later that aside from radio and television announcers, this was not the predominate accent in Brazil which among other things used an aspirated R (like our H in English). It was pretty much business from the beginning, a very old-fashioned text book, really a basic grammar book. Motivation ruled and I got off to a good start. But I never abandoned the idea that the Jesuit father was at Saint Louis U. for other reasons and was "putting in his time" teaching a bit of his native language, perhaps in exchange for board and room, or another degree, who knows. Unlike the entire thrust of my later teaching (and that of the times), I do not recall any meaningful or serious moments when he discussed Brazilian culture. But we learned the language. It was a matter where best friend and colleague Dan Hayes and I studied, practiced speaking ceaselessly outside of class, and in later years delved into the highlights of Brazilian literature, practicing the craft in Portugal (Dan) and Brazil (me) on Fulbright Grants.

It's amazing how one remembers small but important things. It was the day of the Portuguese 101 final exam after a serious semester of study. Dan, or maybe me, said, "You want to go get a beer after the test?" It turned out to be many beers and a long night trying out our rudimentary knowledge of Portuguese. A life-long friendship would ensue. Dan is the "spice" of parts of this narrative. It would become Curran and Hayes, the ant and the grasshopper.

There is yet another aside to be placed here. So much of this story will have to do with Dan Hayes, for he was my "partner" in crime in studies, beer drinking and shared vocations for over three years. There were probably six to seven students in our NDEA class at Saint Louis that year, but I was closest to Dan and we had many, many classes together and experiences shared. But we were unalike in most every way, brain power the main one. I believe today that Dan was near genius level and in fact would be one of SLU's most brilliant graduate students. We were both on the NDEA Fellowship, initially a three-year program. The grant paid tuition and a stipend for books, room and board and incidentals. We were paid once a semester, so it amounted in those days to a

116

fair hunk of change. The ant received his check, deposited it in the bank, paid the semester's board and room and bought books. The grasshopper had other plans.

I was headed into the Pius XII Vatican Library for another study session; it must have been in the p.m. Dan walked around the corner headed for the same place, but with a bit of downcast demeanor. He said, "It's all gone." It turns out he and a good friend thought they had developed a system for the craps table. The friend had gone to Las Vegas a couple of weeks earlier, enrolled in a dealer's school, but with the plan. Dan sent him his entire fellowship check. Crap systems being what they are, Dan that day had his hands full of books but empty of cash the rest of the term.

This all indirectly had to do with that Portuguese 101 class. My friend would arrive Monday morning reeking of body odor, smoke and alcohol. The solution to the lost-grant money was to rack the pool table and tend bar in a St. Louis institution, the Sunday bar. It opened 12:01 Sunday morning and was open for business until midnight Sunday night. I spent some time there, but think it was limited to pool and a couple of beers. Dan bartended and slept in the bar that night, sleeping he said on the pool table. (Shades of W.C. Fields in his younger days). But you noticed the smell which did not affect his intellectual prowess at all. The Sunday "gig" got him by until the grant check the next January. But we launched our future studies, travels and adventures in Portuguese with that class.

Area Studies started the first year. "The South American Indian" and kinship studies in Anthropology bored me to death, putting in my time and surviving the course. A Latin American Politics course was wonderful and provided the basics, but what I recall most was the lay professor's methodology: long, long review lists with names, terms and topics for the exams. Master them and you had an A. I liked the methodology enough to use it in certain undergraduate classes at Arizona State University.

Mark J. Curran

Father John Bannon, S.J., History, Saint Louis University
Courtesy of Saint Louis University, Libraries, Special Collections

The highlight and gift of that first year was Latin American History. Saint Louis University possessed, in this case, a world level scholar. A writer of important books on the history of the Spanish Southwest and of Latin America, Jesuit Priest John Bannon gave us our money's worth. For openers, I was not on a first name relationship with the man, much less a mentor relationship. I doubt he would recognize me in the hallway. But could he lecture! I suppose he may have had some notes, but I never saw them. But for 50 minutes three times a week he enthralled us with both witty and serious commentary, really "telling the story" of Latin America. Had I been a history major, no doubt there would have been a mentor relationship, but I'm grateful for the opportunity and the experience. The methodology was simple: read the textbook, come to class, listen to the lectures, take good notes, study for the long essay exams and hope you understand and remember something. I think this methodology agreed with me and I would adopt much of it, I think a basic of the Jesuit system of those days, for a later career. The main difference in methodology as time went by was at ASU we worked furiously to add "audio-visual" cultural bits to help make our lectures come to life, i.e. documentary films, slides, and perhaps music, but all in a very serious, goal oriented fashion. In 1963 in John Bannon's class it was lecture and listen.

There was a requirement for yet another foreign language in my Ph.D. program, even though Spanish and Brazilian Portuguese were an integral part of the plan. So during that first year at Saint Louis I opted for French, did some study on my own and a few weeks of required classes before taking the French Translation Exam. I am sure it was a "low pass." Enough said.

118

5.   Daily Routine the First Year

There is nothing earthshaking here, but small anecdotes do describe the university life at SLU in the early 1960s. Classes were held, at least in my case, in three or four main buildings around the quadrangle, these buildings I think were original with the campus which publicized itself as being the oldest university west of the Mississippi, perhaps as early as 1818. Anyway the buildings dated from the 19th century, were three or four stories high, red stone on the outside with wooden floors throughout.

Davis-Shaughnessy Hall, Saint Louis University
Photo by Bradley Arteaga, Courtesy of Saint Louis University, Copyright 2011, SLU

There was a small student café we all went to between classes for coffee and to smoke cigarettes. On one such occasion friend Dan Hayes accidentally put out his cigarette on the back of the hand of the young East Indian waiter. Expecting the worst, we all were a bit taken aback when the fine young man just smiled and said "A little suffering is a very good thing."

For the first one or two years anyway, there was a small grocery story-deli where dozens of us would wait in line for the big sandwich and bottle of soda that would become lunch. I would sometimes see Carolyn my nurse friend and her friends there.

Pius XII Library, Dubourg Hall, Saint Louis University
Photo by Bradley Arteaga, Courtesy of Saint Louis Universty, Copyright 2011, SLU

The Pius XII University Library in contrast to the buildings described was sparkling new, a glass and brick structure, very handsome but clashing with the original architecture of the school. It was this building that held the "Vatican Library" with some important manuscripts and papers. I might as well have had a rented room in the library for the many waking hours there studying or attending classes.

St. Francis Xavier College Church, Saint Louis University
Photo by Bradley Arteaga, Courtesy of Saint Louis University, Copyright 2011, SLU

The St. Francis Xavier College Church was patterned on the Gothic of Europe, was built of a whitish stone, with a tall, tall nave running into the transept. I remember the many huge gothic columns, the banners hung from them and the beautiful main altar. There were side chapels and the old fashioned confessionals among them (we still went to confession in those days and there was a nearly deaf old Jesuit that became everyone's favorite: keep it simple, to the point, no questions asked, three Our Fathers and three Hail Mary's). I think we divided time for Sunday mass obligation between the big church and a modern chapel in one of the dorms on Lindell Avenue. It was in the latter that the "folk" mass of the 1960s, post-Vatican II took place. It was new and popular at the time, and it was at this time that the new church music was being composed, not the least by a group which gained national fame, "the Saint Louis Jesuits."

What sticks in my mind was "the prayers of the faithful," a new insertion in the liturgy after the sermon when the public was allowed to add an individual prayer "out loud." Dan Hayes nervously piped up one Sunday: "Oh Lord, Grant that I may find a vein of pure gold in my back yard." Embarrassed silence and a few chuckles followed. This prayer and a few others of the sort, as far as I know, went unanswered by a discriminating Lord.

Mark J. Curran

6. The Neighborhood

Saint Louis University, like many of the big Jesuit schools, is an urban university, located at that time in "Mid-town St. Louis." The core campus was as described with class room buildings, the big administration building, modern dormitories and an old, tiny gym (where we all would thrill to the words of Martin Luther King in a packed house.) A bit to the north was prestigious Lindell Avenue leading to the west and passing by the huge Scottish Rite Masonic Temple, and farther west the St. Louis Cathedral famous for the mosaic scenes and ceiling. It seems funny to me today to consider the Masonic Temple sandwiched between a Jesuit University and a major Catholic Cathedral, but maybe not. Lindell eventually continued to Forest Park, the jewel of St. Louis with a major art gallery, botanical gardens and the Chase Park Plaza Hotel at its edge. In my second year at Saint Louis, the Latinos decided to have a bit of a party at the Chase, everyone putting in some bucks to rent the rooms for the party. I arrived at the party with a date; we danced a bit and left. Later that night much damage was done to the room and we were all called on the carpet and asked (ha!) to pony up for the expenses or face much more serious consequences. Thus ended any connection I had to the Chase Park Plaza.

Forest Park, as mentioned, an immense expanse of green, housed among other things a zoo and a famous art museum. The park would be the site of the world's fair in the 1920s in this "The Athens of the West" as local native Dan Hayes would remind us all too frequently.

Back at SLU, the main north-south street was Grand Avenue and smaller streets, Pine and Olive, and the large Lindell Avenue ran east-west. The major complex of university hospital, nursing school and the rather famous Saint Louis University Medical School were all much farther south on Grand Avenue. And the school of technology and engineering was in fact east of the Mississippi River in Illinois.

In 1963 the city of St. Louis was in the process of urban renewal, badly needed in mid-town due to the poor neighborhoods which were located north and east of the university. In fact SLU had helped the city by developing a small "campus" east of Grand Avenue and I understand, helping with financing of apartments, some school buildings etc. I understand today the area is really quite developed. There is a new basketball arena since my days. Our team played basketball in the old St. Louis Hawks arena.

The area immediately north of campus was a bit dicey, and farther on north through a poorer district was Sportsman Park, the last home of the St. Louis Cardinal Baseball team. In my first year at SLU, in the last years of Stan Musial and Red Schoendienst, I sat with some buddies in the right field bleachers to see Stan the Man get some of his final base hits. More than one young

SLU undergraduate was mugged on the way to the stadium for a ball game in those days; it was best to take a taxi.

At mid-town for perhaps three or four blocks north of the university, there was in fact a viable and distinctive movie-theater district with two or three of the famous glorious "big-time" movie houses dating back to the beginnings of the twentieth century. One theater I recall, the Fox, was extremely ornate with an orchestra pit with a huge player-organ which would rise up on its elevator for live performances before the show, descending once the film began (it was this theater where I took my date Carolyn Schumacher to see the first James Bond film.) And across from that theater was yet another, this one in my mind linked to orchestra performances and the like.

Pine street immediately to the west of the campus was surrounded with old houses, many holding student apartments, but it was Olive Street that most stands out in the memory of most SLU students in the 1960s. There were several student "institutions" on that street, major and minor, which merit a telling.

First of all there were the vagrants hanging out on the street corners and in the smelly, dark doorways. One time Dan Hayes totally emptied his pockets for one of them, quoting as he did a biblical phrase. His knowledge of the Bible by the way was formidable with hundreds of verses memorized, and this all prior to becoming Catholic. "The left hand must not know what the right hand is doing" or something like that. But the vagrants made me nervous; Abilene did not have them, and few lived close to Rockhurst in the 1960s.

The most popular student hangout on Olive was Garivelli's, a jammed, eating place with tiny booths upstairs. The food, as per the name, was "down home" Italian, ravioli, meatballs and pasta, and always with a huge beef for delicious roast beef sandwiches. And you could get a draft beer to wash it down. It sticks in my mind a plate of basic pasta and meat sauce and a hunk of bread was 35 cents. I know it got me by a time or two. But the waiters were not into pleasing the customers. (Was Italy going to be like this?) First of all, they were not friendly; the main agenda was to get your order, bring it, watch over you like a hawk until you finished and make room for the next customer. They certainly looked "old country" to me, what did I know? They did speak a lot of Italian. We spent a lot of time there.

For some reason I never frequented the pool hall upstairs a building or two down, this in spite of spending hours in my brother's pool hall in Abilene. Keah's brother Bud said he did help pay the rent there. And he noted that Minnesota Fats had played a tournament in the same place.

On west at the end of the block was a bar-dive where we spent a fair amount of time, I think because Dan Hayes, a part-time bar keep himself, knew the owner. The joint was across the street from the Sunday beer bar already described. This did not keep us from drinking many a beer there.

I would sum it up as the place where "The Queen of the Silver Dollar" of country music fame might hang out.

The east side of Olive east of Grand Avenue was no less colorful. As you walked down the long block to the "cantina"—like Mexican joint, and it was a joint, you had to go by what was called then "The Queer Bar," the "Orange . . ." or something. I don't know if I could ever bring myself to go in that place. There was a young graduate student in the dorm in a room down the hall from me who would "doll up" with lipstick and makeup and head with friends to the bar, inviting me to do the same. "It's fun," he said.

The Mexican Joint was run by, well, a heavy set, rough living Mexican. I recall only certain things: the food was "Mexican" in name but it was not intended to be "fine cuisine" Mexican. It was spicy and it was cheap. The jukebox had a lot of tunes in Spanish, mainly Mexican I think, who remembers? But many nights over a three year period were spent there with Latinos from SLU, and I even took the guitar a time or two and played my very limited six-song repertoire in Spanish. I could do a "Cumparsita" and "Cumbanchero," another solo or two a friend from Honduras liked, and of course an elementary "Malaguena." It was the loud juke box and revelry headed by a medical school guy from Puerto Rico that I remember most. The Latinos were kind enough to the "gringo" because my heart was in the right place. Curiously enough, in all of St. Louis during the three years I spent there this was the only Mexican place we went to. In those days it was the wrong ethnic group—if you were German or better yet Italian the sky was the limit.

Later I'll tell of a much more respectable social life with great friends from graduate school, the "guys and gals" at parties at the girls' apartments.

In my first or second year in St. Louis, the renowned Gaslight Square was still the "in" place, although it soon decayed, and badly, being in a marginal part of town. And I think the river front development movement of the late 60s was the final straw to break its back. But for me for a year or two it was terrific. Places ranged from fine local restaurants with "singing waiters" who did light opera and Broadway show tunes to true folk music bars with tunes of the times. There was one place with a flamenco guitarist which was of particular interest to me in those days.

And I may be jumping ahead, but there was a memorable evening spent with graduate students from the Hotel Coronado Dorm at Trader Vic's down on the river front. We drank Mai Tais with six kinds of rum. It challenges the memory, now and then, to remember.

7. The Graduate Club

Yet another memory of social life at SLU during my first year was a long-time institution called the Graduate Club. There were no dues, no meetings, no lectures, no debates, but there was a once a month beer blast and dance at a hall rented by the club. The Graduate Club arranged for a keg or two of beer, a stereo system with a couple of speakers, and someone at the door to charge admission and to stamp your hand. Whether desperate or socially inclined, all manner of university graduate students would fill the hall. There were Philosophy and Theology majors, the Business Crowd, the Law School and even Medical school graduate students. And the nurses also showed up.

The president was a very social kid from Rockhurst days, Dick Shaw. He would graduate and return to Rockhurst as a very popular professor for many years. (Dick and his good friend Steve Prengle had taken me under their wing at Rockhurst for entertainment shows and the infamous Liggett and Meyer Cigarette job). Dick lassoed me into becoming an officer (there were no elections), so for a few months I was involved with the deal. I think the rented party halls were American Legion, K of C, Eagles or the like and were in the suburbs of the city. A main memory was hearing the blaring speakers of the stereo set with "It's a Hard Day's Night" of the Beatles. I bought that album by the group, my only one.

8.   Mixers

The Catholic institution was carried on at Saint Louis University. I recall really wanting to meet a good looking co-ed so I attended a mixer early in the fall of my first year at SLU. It was convenient to say the least, held in a parking lot right outside my dorm room. It was there I met a delightful young student-nurse, Miss Carolyn Schumacher from Effingham, Illinois, and we would date off and on for three years. It was a semi-virtuous relationship, giving credit to Carolyn for that, but my raging hormones (and hers too, up to a point) kept the car windows steaming in those cold St. Louis winters. Carolyn would be an important part of my days at SLU.

9. Vacations and Breaks

The NDEA program did not require summer school and it was a good thing. We all needed a break from the intensity of it all. So between my first and second year of graduate school, I drifted back to Kansas City. I cannot recall many details, but I evidently "pounded the streets" hunting for a place to play music. I ended up at an Italian place whose name explains the location, "The 50-50 Club" at 50th Street and . . . , the exact street name escapes me. It was not far from the Plaza, but the place explains the times.

I would play from 9 p.m. to 1 a.m. six days a week, earning the grand total of $50 dollars per week plus all the Italian food I could eat. I don't think the owner threw in drinks on the house, but the customers took care of that. Since I was living rent free with my brother in his place on the Kansas side and had the fellowship in the fall at Saint Louis, the small salary and a few tips were adequate.

It was a learning experience and a growing experience in more ways than one. I sang folk songs, early rock n' roll, cowboy ballads and the like from the 1960s and from midnight to one a.m. would play classical guitar music. Since I had no music system, we made do with a microphone which would pick up the voice and guitar. I believe that the daily routine forced me to expand my singing repertoire to more than 200 songs, and I could do an hour of classic guitar.

The customers were locals, a few bar flies to be sure, but also some buddies from Rockhurst days who would cheer me on. But the main reason I lasted a least a couple of months at the strenuous routine was that there was a Peace Corps Training Group preparing for Honduras taking place at nearby University of Missouri, Kansas City. They would come in, exhausted from the rigorous language and area studies training each day, and relax for a while with a few beers and friendly music. The times were right therefore for the folk tunes and a hootenanny atmosphere, and the volunteers studying Spanish appreciated my few tunes in that language plus the selections of Spanish guitar music.

There was one small technicality: the city was an entertainment hot spot and thus there were "agents" from ASCAP who expected union work and/or fees. Since I was unaffiliated, as it were, the Italian owner said "Don't worry about it. I'll take care of it." And he did. A postscript to that experience: the 50-50 Club had burned down twice. The talk was insurance was duly collected and life went on. Any inference or connection to an Italian organization in the city is unintentional.

As the summer went on, the fun turned into a grind, why not, six nights a week? All good things come to an end. The Peace Corps Training Program ended and my fun audience vanished. Only the barflies remained. And one night when I found myself with a row of about eight drinks on the shelf beside the microphone; it occurred to me that this might not be a good direction to be heading in. My brother Jim inadvertently saved the day, or night, when one evening he came in and said, "I'm going to the Ozarks tomorrow; want to go fishing?" I closed the guitar case, gave notice and thus ended singing and a picking for forty years. I would take up the hobby again only in retirement.

But it was not all socially a waste of time. There were fun moments with the buddies from Rockhurst; the Peace Corps kids were great and a cute blonde waitress helped me pass the time.

Up to this point, as mentioned only briefly, I indeed did have transportation from Abilene, to Kansas City and to St. Louis and back and forth on vacations. It was a 1957 Ford Fairlane blue and white hardback, a four door I think. It did not run well, but lasted until the third year when it limped into St. Louis never to return to the plains of Kansas. I bought it (cheap) at a used car lot in Abilene with earnings from the summer work at the ice plant in Abilene, a job described in great detail in Part I. Two or three strange things: I parked it in the dormitory parking lot behind Griesidieck Hall, but sometimes two or three weeks would go by before I used it, always fearing a rundown battery. The few times I would go home to Mom and Dad in Abilene, perhaps Thanksgiving, Christmas or Easter, but less so as time went by, I would drive the Fairlane. I always stopped in Kansas City to see the ole' Rockhurst buddies, Jim Fitzgerald, Don Brown and especially Bill Rost, of the "Slim and Curly" variety show. Bill and his wife were so good to me; there was always a place on the divan to rest a tired and perhaps a bit tight head. Good times. And there was the time I decided I would THIS TIME make it from St. Louis to Kansas City on one tank of gas. I think the walk to the gas station turned out to be a half-mile, and one learned the true capacity of the Ford gas tank. Upon learning I would be spending a year in Brazil doing fieldwork and research, I gave the car to Jo Anne and Tori Cusack, and it finally "died" the following year. There was a time I took it to a one-armed mechanic over on Pine Street, complaining of a lurching engine; he just smiled sadly and maybe kicked a tire or two.

TIME PASSES—THE SECOND YEAR IN RESIDENCE AT SLU.

1.   Classes, Jesuits and Lay Faculty

As the Ph.D. academic program intensified, now with truly specialized courses, study and hard work ensued. A short perusal of these newest classes and faculty clarify much of the thrust of the program.

Dr. Edward Sarmiento.

This was the outstanding professor who not only taught us, but encouraged us, a true graduate professor. We never got the full story, but it was understood that his roots were in Spain, later in Colombia, and finally in England. Some said he was a "converso" of Jewish roots but converted to Catholicism. I do not know and do not think it matters. I do know he was a daily attendant at mass in the College Church. In spite of being a native speaker of Spanish, he taught all the graduate courses in the Spanish program in King's English; I suspect he could have given lessons to the King and Queen themselves! He said, "The students in the United States are not up to or ready for lectures in Spanish." I think he may not have given us due credit, but be that as it may, he gave outstanding courses. First of all, his knowledge was impeccable, among his claims to fame a concordance on the entire works of the Golden Age poet Garcilaso de la Vega, and secondly, translations from Spanish to English of many of the "Generation of 27," the most famous Spanish poets of the twentieth century, this I think by virtue of several of them living in voluntary exile in England due to the Franco Regime.

Time has passed, but his deliberate, methodical instruction on the nuances of Spanish poetry still is with me. He taught Romanticism espousing still the wisdom of E. Allison Peers, the greatest of critics of that movement, as his guide. He taught Golden Age Poetry and we had demanding courses on Garcilaso de la Vega, Spain's greatest Renaissance poet and Luis de Góngora, the "Prince of Darkness" and perhaps Spain's greatest Baroque poet. And he taught 20th century Spanish poetry, excelling in explanations of text of Federico García Lorca, Pedro Salinas and the rest. In the end, I specialized within the Spanish curriculum in the Golden Age, and his guidance on the poetry of that great age formed my foundation. My class notes from those years guided me in preparation for the survey courses at Arizona State University on the matter.

But there is another more important event related to Dr. Sarmiento. In these years we also studied Latin American Literature, and one very important course was "Modernismo" or the Spanish American Modernist Poets. The class professor, Carlos Lozano, a master in his own right, told me at one point that I should not be in the program. Maybe it was my less than stellar paper on the famous Colombian poet, Guillermo Valencia, and his poem "The Camels" ["Los Camellos"] that caused the professor to utter such a statement. Devastated, I went to Professor Sarmiento who knew me and my work well. He countered the Modernist professor saying I had started slowly (he used to chide me for the farm upbringing and wanted to know all about "corn" and "maize" contrasting the European and American nomenclature) but was making great progress and to pay no attention. I followed his advice. The end of the story, as Paul Harvey might say, was that in 1967 at the Modern Language Association convention in Chicago (lovingly called "the Meat Market") where I interviewed with many fine schools before selecting Arizona State University, the same professor of Modernism, now teaching at a small, Catholic Liberal Arts College in California, offered me a job!

One course may explain my diligence in Professor Sarmiento's classes. The Spanish Baroque poet Luis de Góngora is probably the most challenging and difficult of all poets in Spain. We spent an entire semester with Professor Sarmiento reading his works. I have told this story many times to literature students at ASU: I needed an entire table in the library to prepare for class. One needed the poetry itself in an anthology of Góngora's works, a dictionary of Spanish—English, a Spanish dictionary, a prose translation of Góngora's verse, and then a special dictionary of "Gongorismos," the poet's particular use of poetics, and more which I do not recall. I dug in, persevered and really came to understand the verse. As I think now, when they speak of challenges for the Ph.D. this was close to the top tier.

A short aside: I am positive no graduate school in the United States could have provided the excellence in courses we received at Saint Louis University at the time. We may have not had the Nobel Prize Winners, "Nobeles" as they say in Spanish, such as Stanford, Berkeley or Harvard, but we had fine teachers. Colleagues in later years shared with me that the "famous" public universities with the professors with long lists of publications never guaranteed good instruction in the classroom. It was not that Saint Louis University was shy of such folks, particularly in the School of Medicine or in Liberal Arts as Professor Bannon and Walter Ong remind, but Modern Languages was a teaching faculty par excellence.

There were other professors, but two in particular stand out.

Doris Turner

The first was Doris Turner who taught several courses in Brazilian Literature while an ABD at Saint Louis. Beginning my second year of graduate school Doris would teach Introduction to Brazilian Literature, Machado de Assis, Brazilian Novel and the Novel of the Northeast. She had just returned from a Fulbright Dissertation year in Brazil doing research on the novelist Jorge Amado, would finish the Ph.D. and teach her entire career at Kent State University in Ohio, including heading their Latin American Studies Program. Her Brazilian Portuguese, steeped in Bahia, was like night and day from Fr. Rossi S.J. from southern Brazil. Hers was the accent I would learn gradually in the U.S. and "master" in Brazil in 1966-1967. She took us through our paces with colonial Brazilian Literature, the Romantic period and its poets like Castro Alves, and 20th century masters like Manuel Bandeira and Carlos Drummond de Andrade, as well as 19th century Realism, Naturalism and the Novelists of the Northeast. Strangely enough it was the course on Machado de Assis, perhaps Brazil's greatest "classical" novelist that proved most challenging and intellectually stimulating. We read five or six of Machado's novels and came to appreciate and understand this mixed blood writer of humble beginnings who would be the first President of the Brazilian Academy of Letters.

But there was one class day that changed my life. Doris brought to class that day, in a course where we were introduced to and read novels of Jorge Amado, the best known and best-selling of Brazilian writers up to that point, a handful of Brazilian chapbooks, the story-poems of Brazil's "string literature ["literatura de cordel"]. I'm not sure of her own opinion of them; I believe she saw them more as a curiosity piece, but after explaining a bit about them she suggested they might be of interest to me/us for future research in Brazil. Perhaps she appreciated my rural farm background, interest in folk songs and the like, I don't know. But when it came time to pursue the dissertation, I decided on a topic which would become a lifelong vocation—the "cordel" itself and its relation to erudite Brazilian literature. Encouraged by Doris and others, I made a rather messy application for a Fulbright Hays Grant to Brazil for dissertation research, won the grant, and would spend more than a year in Brazil in 1966-1967 doing the research. So you never know what seeds may be planted and then produce fruit. I always gave Doris credit, but I am sure she had not planned for such an outcome that one day.

**Father Rosario Mazza, S. J. Director of the Department of
Romance Languages, Saint Louis University**
Courtesy of Saint Louis University, Libraries, Special Collections

Father Rosario Mazza, S.J.

A final professor also marked my life but in a much different way. I speak of Father Rosario Mazza, S.J., Director of the Spanish Graduate Program during my time at SLU and a professor of Golden Age Spanish Literature. An Italian-American from Trinidad, Colorado (Italian immigrants to Pueblo and Trinidad were the mainstay of the workers in the steel factories in the former), he joined the Missouri Province of Jesuits and would serve at SLU until his death a few years after I left St. Louis.

He epitomized for me, then and now, the Jesuit tradition, the Jesuit ways. He was first of all a Jesuit priest, but he was an excellent educator, I think exemplifying the education excellence the order was known for. An aside: Recall it was my mother's great respect for this excellence that caused her to encourage her three sons to pursue studies in Jesuit schools: Jim at Creighton in Omaha, Tom at Marquette in Milwaukee and me at Rockhurst College. From the beginning it was clear I was not Father Mazza's favorite student, and for good reason; there were many brighter than I, with better "credentials" and I suspect, possibilities. But he took a chance on the Kansas farm boy of public school education, but with good marks on the undergraduate level at Rockhurst. As I may have mentioned before, but want to emphasize now, I am positive the swaying point for his accepting me in the program with an NDEA grant was an outstanding recommendation from my undergraduate Spanish professor, a layman at Rockhurst, Mr. Vernon Long, who had so highly recommended me for the graduate program and the NDEA fellowship.

Time has blurred the memories but I fancy I had at least three or four courses in the Spanish Literature major from this priest. He was loved but feared by all of us. He was a scholar who published little—how could you when one considered the heavy teaching load he invariably carried, the duties as Jesuit priest, but mainly the demands of an administrator as well? But he read and was "on top of" the intellectual trends of the times—Marshall McCluan's theories, the historical importance of Parry and Lord's research, and colleague Father Ong's pioneering research in literature, among them. There was no end of mimeographed handouts on the latest literary theories.

But he was above all a terrific classroom teacher with the dramatic demeanor that at times goes with it. Appearance was part of it: the quintessential "Black Robe"—stiff white collar, black robe and the belt all the Jesuits kept adjusting perhaps over a protruding belly! He smoked in class, and his language was blue! It caught our attention! There were wonderful lectures spiced with that language, but often with literary asides, philosophical and theological queries, and jokes. And of course there were some sarcastic comments on the times. He classified the students: "Curran is such a goodie-goodie that one day he will be helping a little old lady cross the street and she'll stab him with her umbrella!" Goodie-goodie I was not, but naïve and innocent, yes! Life would have been easier had I a much thicker skin! The priest was "right on."

Father Mazza took us to intellectual and emotional heights dramatizing the antics of Don Quixote! And he pushed us to a reading of most all the great Spanish playwrights from Lope de Vega to Calderón de la Barca, and José Zorrilla, among others, the source for many of the great operas of Italy. A careful reading of the text was first and primary; articles of criticism were secondary and meant to clarify when necessary. This approach to literature, the soaring lectures and hard work approach would become my model for a long career at Arizona State University.

At this point I have to add what happened years later. After the dissertation research, the job beginning at ASU, and the articles and books that followed, I faithfully sent copies to him. I remember only part of his answers; there were not many, but he said, "We never know (speaking of the time in the classroom, exams,) who will excel." What he did not say, was, perhaps, "We did not expect much from you." But maybe not. In due course I will explain his role in the challenging comprehensive exams after the course work, and his indirect direction of my Ph.D. dissertation, another story.

2. Social Life and Good Times

In those final two years in residence there was an active and truly happy social life, all very Catholic, and I suspect very typical of the times.

Social life was good, frequent and fun. On the one hand I dated Carolyn the RN studying for a B.S. degree and we had many good times. There were movies, but one of our favorite things was to go to a jazz bar near Union Station where over beers we would listen to piano, bass, etc. "cool" jazz, the only time in my life I did that. But it was the company that counted. A highlight of our dating was I think my third year when Carolyn invited me to the big Nurses' Ball held at Union Station. It was a beautiful setting and a good time. She was from Effingham, Illinois, the daughter of a successful farmer, and I suppose if things had continued I would have visited the family. It did not get that far, and things changed when I met Keah Runshang during that third year.

Recreation. Graduate Students of Modern Languages and Friends

The Guiness Chorus, Saint Louis University

Another aspect of social life was different but great fun. Many of the girls in the M.A. program in English, French and Spanish had apartments off campus and they threw parties on many weekends. I think of Jeannie Giese to whom I still owe much because she corrected by English in the dissertation and really "fined tuned" it for final production. There was Mary Ann Tinnel, a French M.A. major and a lively girl from back East. Sue Maillou a cheery, exuberant French major was in the middle of it all as were Jo Anne and Tori Cusack, the sisters from Cascade west of Colorado Springs, transfers to Saint Louis U. from Rosary College in Chicago. We became great friends. Jo Anne married and lived many years in Nacogdoches, Texas. Tori married one of the SLU guys, this after I had gone on to Brazil and to Arizona State. She lives an artist's life in Boulder, Colorado, in present days.

The parties were innocent but uproariously fun. There was a lot of beer and wine consumed, and great singing, much of it with my guitar as accompaniment. I recall most of the girls including Jeannie, Jo Anne, and Tori had terrific voices and could harmonize. We sang the folk music of the era. A highlight was a well-oiled Dan Hayes singing an off-tune version of "Folsum Prison Blues." And Jorge Negrete, a graduate student in the School of Medicine and I one bleary night invented and sang a bawdy Mexican ballad ["corrido"], "The Ballad of Felipe Bermejo" in which we included every swear word we both knew in Spanish:

Yo soy Felipe Bermejo, el que robó tanto amor, y cuando vino el sherife, casi murí de terror. pinche Sherife Pendejo, chinga tu madre cabrón; eres un hijo de puta y comes caca cabrón."

Or something like that. Mario Santizo colleague in the Spanish program and friend from Guatemala heehawed at our efforts.

Many a night we spent line dancing to the Zorba the Greek music; great fun, great camaraderie and great memories.

And reflecting upon those times, it was the heyday of the art theater and we spent a few nights out in the suburbs at Clayton where I was introduced to the movies of W.C. Fields which would become a lifelong fascination and some artsy—craftsy stuff by Luis Buñuel including "Viridiana" and "Mexican Bus Ride." And we saw many films from Ingmar Bergman, "Wild Strawberries" and "Through a Glass Darkly" among them. Grass was not our thing (or mine anyway) but many a bleary discussion took place after the movies and beer.

"Hazel Motes' Rat Colored Car," Saint Louis University

We traveled to the parties either in my limp-a-long Ford or Dan Hayes' beat up, wrecked big black Buick. Dan only learned to drive in those years, and the learning curve was steep. This did not keep us from careening around town after way too many beers in the old Buick which could only be entered on the front seat passenger's side. We related it to Haze's (of "Wise Blood" fame) rat colored car, still one of my favorite episodes of the great Flannery O'Connor's prose.

It was at one of these parties at the end of my third year when there was this pretty girl with a yellow or red sweater. Afterwards I asked friend Martha Arms, "Who was that girl?" It turns out it was Miss Keah Runshang, later to become Mrs. Curran, and that was just the beginning of that story.

I must tell of one final episode with the group, a college event so uncommon for me and never repeated, and an event that marks all our friendships. The Ski Trip to Colorado.

I am fuzzy on details, but am sure the idea was born during one of the parties after much beer drinking and all were in good humor. The idea: Hey! Let's go to Colorado to go skiing.

It must have been semester break, the middle of winter. Tori, Jo Anne, Dan Hayes, Jorge Negrete, Mario Santizo, Carol the nurse and who else am I leaving out decided to make the trip. All of us except Jo Anne and Tori were neophytes, never having skied. And Jorge and Mario perhaps had never seen snow. Dan Hayes commandeered the family car ("It has snow tires") and we must have had another. The trek began the first stage with driving to Abilene, Kansas, to my parents' house. I do not know if we spent the night, but we must have, already 450 miles from St. Louis. The second was the drive to Cascade west of Colorado Springs, the home of the Cusacks, a story in itself.

David and Jo Anne Cusack, Cascade House, Colorado

Mark and Jo Anne Cusack, Pre-Ski Talk

Once again, it has been a long time and my facts are fuzzy. The huge beautiful house, really a mansion, was a result we were told, of good fortune in the Colorado gold fields by a family relative, perhaps Mr. Cusack, but it also may have been due to one of the aunts who were instrumental at Rosary College in Chicago. It is quite possible these "facts" have no bearing in reality, but they are what I remember forty-five years later. Nestled in the aspen groves in the foothills of the Rockies west of Colorado Springs, it had a plethora of rooms, but the huge living room was the highlight with a fireplace you could stand in and walls and ceilings decorated I think with a stylish nineteenth century motif. So we partied at the house for a day or two, sleeping upstairs in frigid rooms with many down comforters for the cold. I recall drinking, singing, and talking in front of that huge fire place. The hospitality of Jo Anne's and Tori's parents and aunt had no bounds.

The plan was made and we set out another day in what turned out to be a blizzard. Dan at that time had little experience in driving in the snow, so I think I drove most of the way. We were in white out conditions all the way to Fairplay and then north to Breckinridge. The day's skiing was fun, many took spills, and I just remembered, one of the girls, Carol, broke her leg on the first run. Bummer. But as Terry Thomas said in "It's a Mad, Mad World," we all pressed on!

That night due to low funds and whatever else, we "pressed on" literally to Leadville where we piled into an old, dilapidated hotel where we split rooms, maybe $5 a night per person. Never before or since had I seen such a scene: Leadville was a snowy ice palace (I think of the scene at the old mansion of Dr. Zhivago's family in the film when he wrote the beautiful love poems to Laura.) The ice on the streets was several inches thick and the temperature sub-freezing but this did not keep us from walking the streets to a warm pub where a good time was had by all.

Before the Slopes

The next day we skied again, this time at Cooper Hill, the place, someone said, where the U.S. trained its snow troops in skiing during WW II. Good times. I do not recall anything at all of the drive back to St. Louis, but it was one of those times that will not be repeated . . . ever! And as far as I know, all took place in the highest standards of good Catholic upbringing and morality of the times.

THE FINAL YEAR

1. The Coronado Hotel and Graduate Dormitory

In St. Louis the Jesuits always in need of room for growing enrollment and expansion had purchased two major hotels for dormitories. They were great locations and renovation was less expensive than starting anew. One for the girls became Rogers Hall; Keah lived there during her first year at SLU before transferring, first to the University of Arkansas at Fayetteville and then final happiness at George Washington University in D.C.

The second, on Lindell if I'm not mistaken, was a graduate dorm in the old Coronado Hotel, a famous place in Missouri. I am told that in this ornate, beautiful old place Harry Truman had a Missouri inauguration party commemorating his rise to the presidency of the United States. I lived in the Coronado in style in my third and last year at SLU. My roommate was a Philosophy major, a real gentleman, but we were not of similar interests and friends, even though he had a fine stereo set and played wonderful Baroque music—Handel and Bach—and at a low volume. But the philosophy majors were into pipe smoking and discussions that philosophy majors tend to have, this in the cafeteria of the dorm. We did have one night of camaraderie when I accompanied the pipe smokers to Trader Vic's down on the riverfront where we imbibed sampling the rum concoctions with perhaps five, six, or seven types of the stuff in one huge happy drink. Again, a good time was had by all.

My wonderful memories of the building were of the incredibly ornate lobby all done in fine woods where I would plunk down alone at various hours of the evening to practice a quiet classic guitar. (Recall my times in a room with a nice "echo" in the basement of the dormitory at Rockhurst.) This was classier!

One last memory was the evening at supper when a stomach-ache, or so I thought, developed and did not go away. This was a golden opportunity for the graduate medical students to ask questions and poke and probe a bit. It was due to their concern that I was rushed off to university hospital with an inflamed appendix. Whew. Surgery followed, and quick healing, but it all was a bit scary. The healing was highlighted one day when I heard this chicken-like clucking noise coming down the hallway. Sure enough it was the "gang" of friends, Jo Anne, Tori Cusack, Dan Hayes, and Mário Santizo dragging the toy rooster along behind them to cheer up the ole' farm boy. Such memories, though small, made life worth living, as Bishop Fulton Sheen of those times would say.

2. Academics, Exams and Plans for the Future

Time was marching along and with a whole lot more graduate courses under our belts, it was time for the NDEA program crowd to move to the next step, or next steps.

First was what to do about the dissertation (a matter concurrent with long hours spent reviewing and reading for the Ph.D. comprehensives, no small matter at SLU, more on that later.) Through the encouragement of Doris Turner both Dan and I applied for Fulbright Hays Fellowships for graduate research. It is all a bit murky right now but maybe I can clarify. There were two types of Fulbright graduate fellowships, one for those with a B.A., and a second for a "piled on higher" grant for Ph.D. dissertation research. Still enamored of Spain after the courses with Father Mazza, I applied for the grant to Spain and failed to get it, but was offered one for Mexico. In spite of the success of receiving the grant, I had no great ideas for dissertation research at the time for Mexico. So I also applied for Brazil to research the "Literatura de Cordel," those curious booklets of verse discussed earlier, and their relationship to erudite Brazilian Literature. I had to make the decision after getting the Brazil grant; would it be Mexico or Brazil? Such small decisions convert into major life decisions. I chose Brazil and would head off to that country in July of 1967 to spend slightly more than a year. I have a book about that adventure in preparation, "Adventures of a Gringo Researcher in Brazil."

Dan also received the Fulbright, but to Portugal. That is another story I'll only touch upon here. He learned much of Portugal including the still strange to me Portuguese accent, but managed to spend a fair amount of time in Paris which I believe was the true destination. "The world's greatest and most beautiful city," he would say in Rotarian-like tones, sprinkling bits of French into the conversation. We corresponded with crazy letters recounting our exploits. He got to know Paris and Lisbon; I got to know Recife, Bahia, Rio and the backlands. I think he lived the 1960s a bit more than I.

However, before Rio and "cordel" there was a not so minor matter—passing the strenuous Ph.D. comprehensive exams. They consisted in three long days of writing, one on the major, in this case Golden Age Spanish Literature, another on Latin American Area Studies and a third on Luso-Brazilian Studies, the latter two the minors. I spent much of academic year 1965-1966 in the Vatican Library reviewing class notes and, well, cramming on the books on the reading list for the degree. It would be interesting to see those exams today. Paraphrasing the old country song, "I've forgotten more than you'll ever know about . . . them." But I passed.

A Moment of Jest, a Lesser known Jesuit

Dan and his genius must be addressed at this point. In three years of graduate classwork I never saw him take a note in class. A near photographic memory, an incredible bent for philosophy, language and cultural studies, and an amazing insight or understanding of it all were among his fortés. It was understood he would be brilliant in the exams. Let us jump ahead a year or more to the dissertation and degree. Dan said, "*&*&" that shit!" The result was no dissertation and no Ph.D. He would spend the next forty years as a laborer, first on barges on the Mississippi River and then for diverse construction and landscaping companies in St. Louis. He joined the union and became—lost art—a hod carrier. Mixing the mortar for the bricklayers, carrying the hod up ladders and scaffolds, these were his tasks. But at home at night he read Plato, Socrates, French, Italian, English, and yes Spanish and Portuguese classics. And Philosophy. Many a time over these years I have asked Dad about certain writers and works and ideas; his clear understanding and ability to express it never failed to amaze. Dan never wrote anything to be published; his papers in the graduate courses were small jewels. Should he have become a professor and departed this knowledge? He said something one time about a lack of patience to deal with it all, this in spite of teaching basic Latin and Greek part-time later on. So to address the end of the story at Saint Louis University: What to do with Dan? They gave him an M.A. for his troubles.

I would go on to Brazil, do the work, broaden the farm boy's horizons and eventually write the dissertation, short to be sure, graduate and head to Arizona State for 43 years. The year in Brazil was easy; it was afterwards that was the challenge. I'll return to that.

3.   The Final Days, Social Life

There are a few brief notes to complete the stay and times in St. Louis. After the comprehensive exams in Spring, 1966, the government showered the program with some extra dough. So we had tuition and living money for that summer. Dan and I roomed in the shiny Griesedieck Hall in a small, traditional dorm room. It was then I discovered his modus operandi—we were much like the two opposites on the TV program, the sports announcer and the effete neatnik. After a few weeks of wading through Dan's stuff scattered all over the room, one day I dumped a box of laundry soap in the middle of the room and said, "Stay on the other side of that."

The Final Days, Party on the Admiral, St. Louis

The Goddess Minerva Tattoo and Budweiser Man

A Holding-Up of the St. Louis Arch

But fun times continued, swimming at someone's pool in the St. Louis summer heat, hearing patriotic music near the St. Louis Arch on the 4th of July, some serious beer drinking, classes I can only vaguely remember, and a big party on the Admiral Tour Boat on the Mississippi with the girls and guys previously mentioned, "Our gang." One of the times involved Dan introducing me to the dives in old downtown St. Louis and the near beer bars and then accompanying him to get his newest tattoo, an Owl. Athena—Minerva, goddess of wisdom. He took no small pains to display it to us all on the riverboat. On another occasion Bill Bockelman hosted us on the large family motor boat on a trip up the Mississippi and the Missouri at flood stage. And we all went to the top of the newly built St. Louis Arch; we had accompanied its construction for months from campus. Would the ends meet? All these small things brought St. Louis days to an end, another chapter in the odyssey. The end actually came after Brazil and the fall and winter of 1967-68 when life became a bit more difficult, a story I shall relate to close these memories.

4.   A Return to St. Louis but With Trials and Tribulation

It was good, bad and a bit ugly. After the wonderful year in Brazil which I recount in another book, I returned with some modest savings from the Fulbright Grant. The plan was to go to St. Louis, leave frugally, write the dissertation, do the defense, make job applications and head off into the academic sunset. The sunset arrived but not without enduring a few sunspots and storms.

I returned to St. Louis in the fall, 1967, to proceed with the plan. I think I was driving my brother's broken down, black Chrysler 300 (one side was beaten in, a result of Jim's many wrecks.) I hunted for a small apartment south of the university; the prices were so high and the places were so dismal that in a few short days I returned home to the nest, that is, the upstairs semi-poor artist quarters in my parents' house in Abilene. I would write the dissertation in a tiny upstairs room. And thus I proceeded. Disciplined, to a point, I spent the days reviewing notes, organizing and beginning the writing. Lots of foul cigarette odor filled the air. The plan was to write a chapter, send it to Father Mazza for approval and proceed. It was arduous and the main thing discovered was that I did not have much to say.

Sanity was saved in that after dinner each evening I would repair to Howie's Friendly Tavern on 3rd street where I joined a bunch of cronies—barflies for more cigarettes, conversation and best of all—the ten cent small beers. A pleasant evening could be had for one dollar. There were a couple of cronies from Abilene High School around, and a few more locals, and in particular the local photographer who was well read, a good conversationalist, and inveterate gossip about town. The months passed, a few chapters were written and mailed off to St. Louis. Then it happened.

My dissertation advisor was switched; there was a new man in Portuguese at SLU, a scholar in his own right, but of a different tone. He was of the new school, steeped in literary criticism and somehow wanted my study on Brazilian folk poetry to be literary. I tried; I tried. Then I made the mistake of calling him "pedantic." The inevitable hit the fan; Father Mazza threatened to throw me out of the program and ordered me to cease and desist, right now! Then it got murkier; details escape me but there was a happy ending. The advisor post went back to Fr. Mazza who somehow or other went along with my writing and after much trial and error the dissertation was approved, modest as it was. I never was a "literary" person, not steeped in Criticism but was a good reporter and analyst of the material. I shall never know if he just finally decided to let me "pass out." He did later do the robing ceremony at graduation which I recall only bits of due to the partying the night before. The rest of the story is an anecdote mentioned earlier. After academic success at Arizona State University, a good teaching record, tenure and steady publications, Fr. Mazza wrote me with the "we never know" letter.

As also mentioned Jeannie Giese saved the day, correcting my English in the dissertation, editing it and perhaps even typing it for the final Xeroxing. I am forever in her debt.

A final note is social. In the final months trying to wrap up the dissertation I would return to St. Louis, board in the house of Dan Hayes' parents, laugh myself sick at all their antics, survive jobs of substitute teaching in the St. Louis inner city schools (nightmares reoccur of those moments), and survive on nickels and dimes until the end. It was in those days that I met Keah Runshang at one of the parties, and we began to date. This continued, off and on, sporadically when I was in town, and she joined me at the graduation ceremony in January of 1969. But I must add to the academic odyssey: in late fall of 1967 while still writing chapters in Abilene, it was time to actually apply for jobs, assuming of course one finished the degree. The way to do it in those days was to apply to schools and set up appointments and do interviews at the Modern Language Convention taking place after Christmas in Chicago.

On a frigid December day in 1967 I took the Union Pacific Train from Abilene to St. Louis, was met by Dan, faithful friend to the end, and he drove us to Chicago in the frigid, icy winter weather and we stayed at the less than stellar LaSalle hotel in the old downtown of Chicago. The MLA Meeting was in nicer lodgings nearby. I had several excellent interviews, one from the University of Nebraska, another by Professor and future boss Herbert Van Scoy from Arizona State University. ASU outbid Nebraska by $200, and that along with the promise of warm weather, spring training baseball, ASU's Latin American Center and proximity to Mexico made his case. We reached an initial agreement, a handshake at the meeting, and it was all sealed curiously enough in those days with a telegraphed offer. Signed, sealed and delivered.

There is just a personal footnote to end those moments. At the same time as the convention in Chicago I had a whopping case of the flu; it was below zero outside, and the drive back to St. Louis was after one of those incredible ice storms in the Mid-West. Dan brought me to St. Louis, I boarded the Union Pacific to Abilene where my dear ole' Dad met me at the station, me miserably sick, to take me to the warm house on Rogers Street, and back to the dissertation routine described earlier. This was the last time I truly felt dependent upon my parents. Reflecting back on those days and events today, a parent myself, I believe I understand parental love and sacrifice.

Mark, Graduation, Ph.D. Saint Louis University, 1969

I actually received the degree in June of 1968 but was required to go back for the formal graduation the next January, already described.

That summer I spent three months laboring for a local Abilene farmer, getting the academic cobwebs out of my brain; it was a thoroughly pleasant experience. I did field work on a big dually John Deere tractor, broke my big toe from a disk that came down a bit too soon, and drank beer at Howie's. In early September, 1968, I drove the old wreck of a Chrysler to Tempe, Arizona, breaking down in Lubbock, Texas, along the way and reported for duty dressed in coat and tie in 100 plus temperatures. Never shall I forget, on the preceding day driving over the last ridge of small mountains near Globe, Arizona, on the way to the Valley of the Sun, the horizon was white with heat. I drove for what seemed like miles before finding a motel on old Apache in Tempe.

The rest is another story. On the academic side, there would be 34 years of full-time teaching at ASU, nine more part-time after retirement, 20 research trips to Brazil, and many articles and books published. Equally or more important, there would be marriage to Keah, the birth of our child Kathleen and a contented life to the present in 2012.

PHILOSOPHIZING BY A NON-PHILOSOPHER

The decision for a title for this book was not an easy one. "Coming of Age with the Jesuits" could just as well have been "Growing Up with the Jesuits." I think one can see that a major undercurrent in the book is the fact it deals with a young man setting off for college at the tender age of 19, four years as an undergraduate, and a wide-eyed first experience outside of the United States at only twenty years of age. The next five years, three in residence at Saint Louis University, a year in Brazil, and a final year with the struggle to write and finish the dissertation and hunt for a job in academia did bring some maturity. For sure it came after settling down in Tempe, Arizona, at Arizona State University in 1968.

So in one sense the Jesuits formed the chorus in this drama, always in the background and certainly filling in the empty spaces. Yet in the big scheme of things, Catholic formation, religious practice and particularly wonderful education and mentoring on the undergraduate level by an outstanding Spanish teacher and the graduate level by Jesuit role models would definitely form my ideas first for a teaching career, but more importantly for growing up and maintaining Catholic traditions in the classroom and life. A thank you is in order. Amen.

ABOUT THE AUTHOR

Mark Curran is a retired professor from Arizona State University where he worked from 1968 to 2011. He taught Spanish and Brazilian Portuguese languages and their respective cultures. He researched Brazil's folk-popular literature, "A Literatura de Cordel," and has published twenty-five scholarly articles and nine books in Brazil, Spain, and the United States on the subject. "The Farm" published in 2010 was a change of pace to the auto-biographical, recollections of growing up on a family farm in central Kansas in the 1940s and 1950s. "Coming of Age with the Jesuits" chronicles seven years in Jesuit college and graduate school and his first forays to Latin America.

Books Published:

A Literatura de Cordel, Brazil, 1973
Jorge Amado e a Literatura de Cordel, Brazil, 1981
A Presença de Rodolfo Coelho Cavalcante e a Moderna Literatura de Cordel, Brazil, 1987
La Literatura de Cordel—Antología Bilingüe—Español y Portugués, Spain, 1990
Cuíca de Santo Amaro—Poeta-Repórter da Bahia, Brazil, 1991
História do Brasil em Cordel, Brazil, 1998
Cuíca de Santo Amaro—Controvérsia em Cordel, Brazil, 2000
Brazil's Folk-Popular Poetry—"A Literatura de Cordel"—A Bilingual Anthology in English and Portuguese, USA, 2010
The Farm, Growing up in Abilene, Kansas, in the 1940s and 1950s, USA, 2010
Retrato do Brasil em Cordel, Brazil, 2011
Coming of Age with the Jesuits, 2012

Curran makes his home in Mesa, Arizona, and spends part of the year in Colorado. He is married to Keah Runshang Curran, and they have one daughter, Kathleen, who lives in Flagstaff, Arizona, and makes documentary films. Her film "Greening the Revolution" was shown most recently at the Sonoma Film Festival in 2012.
Email: profmark@asu.edu
Web page: www.currancordelconnection.com